SHONALI THOMAS

A DOSE OF HEALTHY
INDULGENCE FROM

Shonals'
KITCHEN

Warren Publishing
warrenpublishing.net
Publishing and printed in USA

Photography by Chuck Eaton.
All images copyright by Chuck Eaton Photography.
ISBN: 978-1-943258-47-5

SplenDishes Gourmet Foods is a made-to-order gourmet food service featuring small batch, boutique-style sauces, spice blends, mustards, jams, and jellies, using locally-sourced ingredients. Our foods are preservative-free and most are gluten-free, as well. Our gourmet spice blends are delicious and savory on all kinds of meat, chicken, seafood, and vegetables, and our gourmet condiments are great for get togethers and gift-giving."

BBQ Rub

South O' the Border Blend

Fire Roasted Salsa

Super Tuscan Blend

Bourbon Bacon Salt

Signature House Blend

Pumpkin Pie Blend

Rosemary Lemon Salt

Bacon Marmalade

Cranberry Jelly

Zinful Wine Jelly

Pepper Jelly

CONTENTS

Follow Shonali Thomas

@splendishes

@splendisheskitchen

@shonalskitchen

My name is Shonali, but my closest friends call me Shonals. My friends and family mean the world to me and my eclectic cooking style brings them around the table and into my kitchen.

The last couple years have brought a lot of muses to my love of cooking. From friends who have never tried a certain dish or ingredient, to a fan who watched me make a recipe on one of the several local morning TV shows that I cook on, this book is a celebration of my most loved recipes from friends, family, and my loyal TV followers. From simple to elegant, these dishes are easy enough to be made at home, yet still restaurant-worthy. Each dish is a healthy indulgence the whole family can enjoy.

I love to recreate dishes I've had in restaurants, and I am honored to be able to share recipes from three of my favorites. I am fortunate enough to know the chefs or owners, as well as the bartenders, and have featured their fantastic recipes in the Chef-Inspired sections of this book. I had so much fun playing in the kitchen or behind the bar with each of them!

Being raised in Sonoma County, CA, wine country is close to my heart. Most everyone knows my love for vino! While living in Northern California, I spent a lot of time wine tasting and learning all I could about the wines and how they are made. My recipes often use wine or beer in them, because I find they add so much flavor, so pairing the recipes in this book with wine or beer was only fitting. My good friend Stephen Johnson from Rush Espresso Café and Wine Bar is a Sommelier and gave his suggestions for beer and wine throughout the book.

My daughter, Shaiyla and her love of cooking inspired me to create a Little Chef's Cooking Class. It started at her preschool and has quickly grown to be a #1 After School Enrichment Program in several elementary schools across the Charlotte area. Inspiring young minds to embrace cooking and teaching them about new and sustainable ingredients is so important, and I look forward to all the eager little faces in every new program that starts!

Owning a local gourmet foods business, SplenDishes Gourmet Foods, has given me another opportunity to share my love of food. Over the years, I've created top-selling gourmet sauces, spice blends, mustards, jams, jellies, and salsa. You can find my products in several specialty stores and online. I regularly use several of these items in my everyday recipes and in this book.

When I'm not running my business, teaching my Little Chefs or trading tips with local chefs, I enjoy cooking at home with my husband Eric, (the Grill Master!), and my daughter, Shaiyla.

It's all about great food, fabulous wine, and the best of friends. Welcome to Shonals' Kitchen!

APPETIZERS

Whether it's a catering gig, a cooking party, or my own party, appetizers are always popular. They can be the first impression at a dinner party, or the main attraction for a holiday party or get together. Either way, apps should be simple, yet elegant and easy to eat. Here are a few of my most requested favorites.

Grilled Peaches with Prosciutto & Balsamic Drizzle

Serves approximately 4

4 peaches
8 slices prosciutto, sliced in half, longwise
16 large basil leaves
Extra-virgin olive oil
Balsamic syrup to drizzle
Fresh basil for garnish

1. Cut each peach into quarters. Place 1 basil leaf over top of peach, then wrap securely with a slice of prosciutto and secure with toothpick.
2. Heat grill or grill pan to medium heat.
3. Brush peaches generously with olive oil to prevent the prosciutto from sticking to the grill.
4. Grill peaches until char marks appear, turning peaches until sides are evenly cooked, about 10-12 minutes.
5. Transfer peaches to a platter and remove toothpicks. Drizzle with balsamic syrup and garnish with fresh torn basil.

Want Wine?

Wine pairing suggestion:
Albariño

Wine notes for similiar choice:
Minerality, white flowers, and fruit forward for these wines is a great pairing for the sweet and salty flavors.

Fall Fritters
Makes approximately 15 fritters

6 large croissants, torn into small pieces
1 small sweet yellow onion, finely chopped
2 celery stalks, finely chopped
1 garlic clove, finely chopped
1 tablespoon SplenDishes House Blend
1 teaspoon flat leaf parsley, finely chopped,
   plus extra for garnish
1 teaspoon fresh sage, finely chopped
2 tablespoons olive oil, plus extra for
   shallow frying
½ cup dry white wine
1 egg, beaten
SplenDishes Zinful Wine Jelly

1. In a large sauté pan, heat olive oil on medium
   high heat and sauté onions, celery, and garlic
   until translucent, about 4 minutes. Season
   with House Blend, and stir in fresh herbs and
   wine. Bring to a low boil, then reduce heat
   and simmer for 2-3 minutes, then remove
   from heat.
2. Place torn croissants into a bowl and pour in
   onion mixture, mix until combined. Season
   to taste, if needed. Let mixture slightly cool,
   then fold in egg.
3. Using same sauté pan, heat a thin layer of oil,
   just to cover bottom of pan. Drop mixture
   in tablespoon sized scoops into hot pan.
   Gently flatten with spatula and fry for about
   3 minutes, until golden brown on each side.
   Remove from pan and place on paper towel-
   lined baking sheet. Season with flake salt.
4. Fritters can be re-heated in a 375° F oven
   for 10-12 minutes before serving. Fritters
   can also be served at room temperature.
5. To serve, top with a small spoonful of
   SplenDishes Zinful Wine Jelly, in the center
   of each fritter and garnish with parsley.

Want Wine?
Wine pairing suggestion for Prosciutto-Wrapped Asparagus:
Sparkling Rosé or Red

Wine notes for similiar choice:
The saltiness and dryness is excellent with a Sparkling Rosé or Red.

Prosciutto-Wrapped Asparagus
Serves 8-10

1 pound asparagus spears, trimmed
6 ounces thinly-sliced prosciutto
Extra-virgin olive oil, for drizzling
SplenDishes House Blend

1. Wrap each asparagus spear tightly with a half-
   slice of prosciutto and place on a baking sheet.
2. Once all spears are wrapped, place in
   refrigerator and chill for 30 minutes.
3. Place wrapped asparagus on another baking
   sheet, leaving space in between each one (if
   you crowd the pan, they won't get crispy).
4. Drizzle with olive oil and sprinkle with
   SplenDishes House Blend.
5. Place under broiler for 4-6 minutes, keeping
   a close eye on them so they don't burn.
   Once ends of prosciutto start to get crispy,
   take them out.
6. Serve immediately.

Want Wine?
Wine pairing suggestion for Fall Fritters:
Syrah

Wine notes for similiar choice:
Dark fruits (blackberry) with some smoke flatters this dish.

Goat Cheese & Prosciutto Crostini with Caramelized Onions & Balsamic Syrup
Makes approximately 25 crostini

1 baguette, sliced ¼" thick
2 tablespoons olive oil, plus extra for
   brushing on baguette
Sea salt, for sprinkling
4 ounces goat cheese
4-6 ounces prosciutto
2 yellow onions
Balsamic syrup, for drizzling
Chives, for garnish

1. Preheat oven to 400° F.
2. Place crostini on parchment-lined baking
   sheet, brush both sides with olive oil and
   sprinkle with sea salt.
3. Bake about 3-4 minutes each side, until
   lightly golden and still soft inside.
4. Sauté onions in olive oil on medium heat
   until golden and caramelized, about 10-15
   minutes. (Can be done ahead of time and
   set aside.)
5. Spread goat cheese on each baguette, top
   with prosciutto and onions, then drizzle with
   balsamic syrup over top.
6. Garnish with cut chives.

Want Wine?
Wine pairing suggestion for Goat Cheese & Prosciutto Crostini with Caramelized Onions & Balsamic Syrup:
Oregon Pinot Noir

Wine notes for similiar choice:
The acid helps increase the flavors and cuts the creaminess of the cheese; earthiness pairs well with onions.

Want Wine?

Wine pairing suggestion:
Chenin Blanc

Wine notes for similiar choice:
Aromatic and dry is perfect with seafood; soft acid cuts through the richness of the sauce.

Crab Cakes with Spicy Remoulade Sauce
Makes 8 crab cakes

½ cup mayonnaise
1 egg, beaten
1 tablespoon Dijon mustard
1 tablespoon Worcestershire sauce
½ teaspoon hot sauce
½ teaspoon Old Bay® Seasoning
1 pound jumbo lump crabmeat
20 butter crackers, finely crushed
2-3 scallions, thinly sliced (save some for garnish)
¼ cup canola oil
Lemon wedges, for serving

1. In a small bowl, whisk the mayonnaise with the egg, mustard, Old Bay Seasoning, Worcestershire sauce and hot sauce until smooth.
2. In a medium bowl, lightly toss the crabmeat with the cracker crumbs. Gently fold in the mayonnaise mixture. Cover and refrigerate for at least 1 hour.
3. Scoop the crab mixture into eight ⅓-cup mounds; lightly pack into eight patties, about 1 ½ inches thick. In a large skillet, heat the oil on medium high. Add the crab cakes and cook over moderately high heat until golden brown and heated through, about 3-4 minutes per side. Transfer the crab cakes to plates and serve with lemon wedges.

Spicy Remoulade Sauce

1 ¼ cups mayonnaise
¼ cup mustard (Creole mustard if possible)
1 tablespoon sweet paprika
Pinch of Old Bay Seasoning
1-2 teaspoons Cajun or Creole seasoning
2 teaspoons prepared horseradish
1 teaspoon sweet pickle juice
1 teaspoon hot sauce
1 large clove garlic, minced and smashed

1. Whisk all the ingredients together in a medium bowl. The remoulade is better if left for a few hours to let the flavors meld. Keep refrigerated.

Drunken Shrimp with House-made Hummus in Cucumber Cups
Makes approximately 20 pieces

Pickled Shrimp
1 pound 16-20 count Argentine pink shrimp, peeled and deveined (leave tails on)
3 lemons, juiced and zested
½ cup apple cider vinegar
1 ½ cups white wine
¼ cup extra-virgin olive oil
½ yellow onion, chopped
3 garlic cloves, peeled and smashed
1 teaspoon SplenDishes House Blend

1. Poach shrimp in 2 cups water plus 1 cup white wine until opaque and cooked through, about 4 minutes. Transfer to colander and run under cold water to stop cooking.
2. Combine remaining ingredients in a large bowl, then add shrimp. Cover and marinate for 4 hours or overnight.

House-made Hummus
2 garlic cloves
2 cans chickpeas, drained
2 lemons, juiced
2 tablespoons tahini (sesame paste)
½ teaspoon SplenDishes Rosemary Lemon Salt

1. Combine ingredients in food processor and blend until creamy. Season to taste.
2. Keep in sealed container in refrigerator for up to 2 weeks.

Additional Ingredients Needed
1 English cucumber, cut into ¾ inch slices and top center (seeds) scooped out
SplenDishes Rosemary Lemon Salt
Fresh dill

To assemble
1. Drain shrimp and place on paper towels to absorb excess liquid.
2. Place hummus into pastry bag and pipe into each cucumber cup. Sprinkle a pinch of Rosemary Lemon Salt over each and place a shrimp over hummus. Garnish each with a small sprig of fresh dill.

Want Wine?

Wine pairing suggestion:
Dry Riesling

Wine notes for similiar choice:
Perfect with seafood in general but especially with fresh herbs.

Rosemary Garlic Shrimp
Serves approximately 6

1 pound 16-20 count shrimp,
  peeled and deveined
2 tablespoons fresh rosemary, finely chopped
2 tablespoons fresh garlic, finely chopped
1 tablespoon applewood-smoked seasoning
3 ounces extra-virgin olive oil
Sea Salt, for sprinkling
Toothpicks, for serving

1. Place shrimp in a bowl and toss with
   rosemary, garlic, applewood-smoked
   seasoning, and olive oil. Marinate for 30
   minutes, covered in refrigerator.
2. Place shrimp on very hot grill for 1-2 minutes
   each side, depending on size of shrimp.
3. Place on a platter and sprinkle with sea salt.
   Serve with toothpicks.
4. For a prettier presentation, skewer shrimp
   on fresh rosemary sprigs!

Black Eyed Pea Fritters with Bacon Marmalade
Makes approximately 15-18 fritters

1 onion, diced
1/2 red bell pepper, diced
1 clove garlic, minced
Two (15.5 ounce) cans black-eyed peas
1 tablespoon all-purpose flour
1 egg
1 green onion, sliced, plus more for garnish
1/2 teaspoon cayenne pepper
1 cup fresh breadcrumbs
1/3 cup vegetable oil
1 teaspoon SplenDishes House Blend
SplenDishes Bacon Marmalade

1. Preheat oven to 350° F.
2. Heat 1 tablespoon of the oil in a skillet over medium heat. Add the onion, red bell pepper, and garlic and sauté until soft, about 3 minutes. Reduce heat, add the black-eyed peas and roughly mash all the ingredients together with a potato masher. Remove from the heat and cool slightly.
3. Add the flour, egg, green onion, cayenne, and 1/4 to 1/2 cup breadcrumbs to the pea mixture. Fold in remaining black-eyed peas. Season with House Blend.
4. Place the remaining breadcrumbs in a shallow bowl. Scoop batter into large, tablespoon size portions. Press into flat 1/2-inch-thick discs and coat in the remaining breadcrumbs.
5. Wipe out the skillet. Heat the remaining oil and, in batches, sear the fritters until golden brown, about 2 minutes per side. Place on a baking sheet and finish cooking in the oven until cooked through, 15 to 20 minutes.
4. Top with the SplenDishes Bacon Marmalade and garnish with the green onions.

Want Wine?

Wine pairing suggestion
Black Eyed Pea Fritters
with Bacon Marmalade:
California Pinot Noir

Wine notes for similiar choice:
Red cherry fruit with soft earth and acid praises this dish.

Want Wine?

Wine pairing suggestion for
Baked Brie Trio and Rosemary
Garlic Shrimp:
Viognier

Wine notes for similiar choice:
Floral tones and being fruit forward balances spice and richness.

Baked Brie Trio

3 sheets puff pastry, thawed
3 rounds brie cheese
3 ounces SplenDishes Pepper Jelly
3 ounces SplenDishes Bacon Marmalade
3 ounces Sundried Tomato Pesto
3 tablespoons butter, melted
Toasted baguette, sliced

1. Preheat oven to 400° F.
2. Place each sheet of puff pastry on a greased baking dish, placing brie rounds in the center. Spoon each of the toppings separately over the tops of brie. Bring sides of pastry up and gently wrap, so it's completely sealed.
3. Brush each with melted butter and bake for 25-30 minutes, until golden brown.
4. Serve with sliced and toasted baguette.

QUICK TIP: Prepare ahead (up to the baking part) and keep in fridge until ready to bake.

Bourbon Bacon Fried Chicken
Makes approximately 24 chicken pieces

4 chicken cutlets, cut into 1" x 2" wide pieces
1 ½ cups buttermilk or sour milk*
4 tablespoons Sriracha hot sauce
1 ½ cups all purpose flour
1 tablespoon SplenDishes House Blend
1 teaspoon cayenne pepper
SplenDishes Bourbon Bacon Salt
12 ounces canola oil

To Marinate Chicken
1. Combine buttermilk, Sriracha, and chicken in ziplock bag and marinate overnight (or at least 4 hours). Be sure to take out of refrigerator 30 minutes before ready to fry.
2. Prep Flour Mixture: In a shallow bowl, combine flour, House Blend, and cayenne pepper. Taste and add additional seasoning, if needed. Cover and set aside until ready.
3. Heat canola oil in deep fry pan on high heat until it reaches between 350-375° F.
4. Dredge chicken in flour mixture, shaking off excess flour and gently place into oil. Fry until golden brown, about 6-8 minutes on each side.
5. Remove from oil and place on paper towels and season immediately with Bourbon Bacon Salt.
* To make sour milk, add 1 tablespoon vinegar to 1 cup milk.

Want Wine?

Wine pairing suggestion:
Pinot Grigio

Wine notes for similiar choice:
A dry white wine balances the creamy texture.

Spicy Deviled Eggs topped with Bourbon Bacon Fried Chicken

6 large eggs
2 tablespoons mayonnaise
1 teaspoon Dijon mustard
⅛ teaspoon SplenDishes House Blend
Sriracha hot sauce

1. Place eggs in a single layer in a saucepan; add enough cold water to cover eggs.
2. Bring to a boil; cover, remove from heat, and let stand 20 minutes.
3. Drain immediately and fill the saucepan with cold water and ice.
4. Tap each egg firmly on the counter and peel under cold running water.
5. Using a clean knife each time, slice eggs in half lengthwise, and carefully remove yolks.
6. Mash yolks with a fork, then add mayonnaise, mustard, and House Blend. Using a hand beater, beat on medium-high until fluffy and creamy. Fold in Sriracha to desired level of heat.
7. Using a pastry bag (or ziplock bag with end cut off), pipe yolk mixture into egg whites.
8. Garnish each egg with Bourbon Bacon Fried Chicken.

CHEF-INSPIRED
ILIOS NOCHE

Executive Chef James Jermyn
Ilios Noche

Chef James Jermyn has a bold understanding for his industry. Growing up in a Southern family, he was surrounded by food made with passion and hospitality. James continued his learning during his culinary education at CPCC. He continued his career path, moving to New York City and working at prestigious restaurants such as La Goulue, Orsay, Park Avenue Café, and Maloney & Porcelli. While working in NYC, he gained a deeper knowledge of diverse ingredients.

James took an opportunity to work with Chef Neil Murphy at Park Avenue Café as his Chef de Cuisine, preparing contemporary American menus based on produce from local farms. After taking the executive chef position with Maloney & Porcelli, he created unique culinary ideas with creative flare. He won the Beef Backer Award for the Northeast and earned a nomination for Best Chefs America. He has received accolades from *Daily News, The New York Times, Food Arts, New York Magazine, Grubstreet, The Wall Street Journal,* and *Michelin Guide.* He has also been featured on NBC, NY Live, and NY CBS local.

Ilios Noche is an upscale, Mediterranean-inspired restaurant with two locations in Charlotte, NC. Their chefs, bartenders, and staff are top-notch, and the owner, Stratos Lambos, was kind enough to let me in his kitchen with Chef James Jermyn to make two of my favorite dishes.

Ilios Noche's Greek-style Pork Ribs are like none other you've had before. The rib meat practically falls off the bone, and they feature a tangy coriander-lemon rub, served with a creamy tzatziki sauce. It's no wonder they're a local favorite!

Chef James also gave me an inside look at how to make their amazing flaming cheese. Saganaki, in Greek cuisine, is a dish prepared in a special, small frying pan. The cheese is melted until bubbling and finished with lemon and ouzo. If you don't have a Saganaki pan, don't worry! Any small, non-stick skillet will work!

In addition to cooking, James' goal is to develop young, upcoming chefs to discover their talents and be passionate for the industry that he loves. He tries to impart the sense of hospitality that has been taught to him. James continuously stays active in his community and strives to learn new aspects of his industry on a daily basis.

Bartender Justin Gehman-Arrowood
Justin started working in restaurants when he was 16 years old and has been a bartender, perfecting his craft over the last 10 years.

You can't eat amazing food without amazing wine to go with it! Bartender Justin Gehman-Arrowood shared his delicious Sangria recipe with us. The fresh berry simple syrup really makes this decadent sangria stand out from the rest.

If you're local to Charlotte, or just passing through, Ilios Noche is a must try!

Greek-Style Pork Ribs From Ilios Noche

Serves approximately 8-10 people

6 pounds pork ribs, (about 3 racks of ribs)
1 sliced onion
1 lemon cut into half
1 sprig fresh thyme
5 garlic cloves
Water to cover
Salt and pepper to taste

Coriander rub

6 tablespoons coriander
2 tablespoons lemon zest
Mix together

1. Preheat oven to 350° F.
2. Season pork ribs with salt and pepper.
3. In a braising pan over medium heat, sear ribs on both sides. Once golden brown, add remaining ingredients (except coriander rub) and bring to a simmer.
3. Cover with aluminum foil and place in oven, cook 2 ½ hours.
4. Remove ribs after tender, let cool, then cut rib racks into thirds.
5. Drizzle with olive oil and place on hot grill until lightly charred.
6. Season with coriander rub and serve.

Saganaki (fried cheese) from Ilios Noche

Cut ⅛" thick piece of kefalograviera cheese or
  haloumi Cheese
¼ cup olive oil
½ ounce ouzo
¼ ounce lemon juice
½ cup all-purpose flour

1. In a heavy pan over medium heat, add olive oil.
2. Lightly flour the pieces of cheese.
3. Once pan is hot, place cheese in the oil, and
   sauté until golden brown, and flip to other
   side.
3. Once both sides are brown, pour off excess
   olive oil.
4. Take pan off flame and add ouzo, place pan
   back over flame to burn off alcohol.
5. Add lemon juice and a pinch of salt to taste.
6. Serve in desired dish.

Justin's Signature Sangria

1 bottle of red wine
12 ounces orange juice
12 ounces cranberry juice
4 ounces brandy
10 ounces mixed-berry syrup
Fresh fruit

1. In a large beverage container, combine red
   wine, orange juice, cranberry juice, brandy, and
   mixed-berry syrup. Stir until well combined.
   Garnish with fresh berries and fruit.

Mixed-Berry Syrup Recipe

8 ounces water
8 ounces granulated sugar
1 cup mixed berries

1. In a sauce pan, combine water, sugar, and
   berries. Bring to a boil, then lower heat and
   simmer until sugar dissolves and berries
   break down. Run mixture through a seive
   and keep refrigerated.

ENTRÉES

I love the diversity of an entrée. Whether you're making supper for your family or throwing a dinner party, cooking should be fun and easy. Here are some of my favorite recipes that range from basic to not so basic. From juicy chicken dishes to amazing comfort foods and elegant plating ideas, each entrée provides its own dose of healthy indulgence. Simple steps, simple ingredients, delicious results.

Grilled Artichokes with Lemon Caper Butter
Serves 4

2 Artichokes
Extra virgin olive oil
SplenDishes Bourbon Bacon Salt
8 tablespoons butter
2 tablespoons capers, chopped
Fresh lemon juice
Pinch of SplenDishes House Blend

1. To prep artichokes, cut the bottom stem off, trim sharp ends of leaves, and cut top off to make a flat surface.
2. Steam, top side down, in 1 inch of water for about 35 minutes or until stem is tender when fork is inserted. Let cool for 5 minutes.
3. Using a sharp knife, cut artichokes in half and remove hairy choke and small center leaves.
4. Drizzle with olive oil and sprinkle open-faced and in between leaves with SplenDishes Bourbon Bacon Salt and place in grill pan, heart side down.
5. Place grill pan on hot grill (or stovetop), and cook for about 10 minutes until edges are golden brown.
6. In 4 small bowls, melt 2 tablespoons butter, a dash of lemon juice, pinch of SplenDishes House Blend, and 1 teaspoon of chopped capers. Serve alongside Grilled Artichokes.

Want Wine?

Wine pairing suggestion:
Gruner Veltliner

Wine notes for similiar choice:
Primarily grown in Austria and a good Sauvignon Blanc alternative. Slight spice with some acid and dry.

A fan favorite, I posted this recipe in October, 2013 on social media and within a few weeks the post had gone viral. Since then, it has been viewed over 224 million times, shared over 545,000 times, and there are over 50,000 comments that still come in, to this day!

Crash Hot Potatoes
Serves 4

8 baby red potatoes
¼ cup extra-virgin olive oil
SplenDishes Bourbon Bacon Salt
4 cloves garlic, smashed into a paste
2 tablespoons fresh herbs, finely chopped
  (rosemary, thyme, and oregano work great)
¼ cup grated parmesan cheese

1. Preheat oven to 425° F.
2. Cook potatoes in microwave until fork tender (approximately 3-5 minutes).
3. Combine olive oil, herbs, and garlic in a small bowl.
4. Place potatoes on well-greased baking sheet. Using a potato masher, gently smash down potatoes in a crisscross direction (so it resembles a peanut butter cookie).
5. Brush smashed potatoes generously with olive oil mixture.
6. Bake for 12 minutes, then top with parmesan cheese. Bake an additional 10 minutes, until tops and edges are crispy.

Chicken Asparagus Rolls
Serves 4

4 chicken cutlets, pounded out to ¼" thickness
SplenDishes Bourbon Bacon Salt
8 slices prosciutto
2 tablespoons Dijon mustard
1 bunch asparagus, ends trimmed
3 tablespoons olive oil
Parsley, chopped for garnish

1. Preheat oven to 375° F.
2. Season cutlets with SplenDishes
   Bourbon Bacon Salt.
3. Spread a thin layer of mustard on chicken,
   then lay a piece of prosciutto down.
4. Place 4-6 asparagus spears in center of
   chicken, placing spears to stick out at
   each end.
5. Starting at one end, roll chicken up tightly and
   secure with toothpick. Season again with just a
   pinch of SplenDishes Bourbon Bacon Salt.
6. Heat sauté pan on medium-high heat and
   add olive oil.
7. Place in hot pan, seam side/toothpick up.
   Brown for 4-5 minutes, then flip and brown
   another 4-5 minutes.
8. Transfer chicken to baking dish, place in
   oven, and bake for 20-25 minutes.
9. Let chicken cool about 5 minutes. With a
   very sharp knife, slice chicken diagonally, in
   half. Garnish with chopped parsley.

Want Wine?

Wine pairing suggestion:
Chardonnay

Wine notes for similiar choice:
*Creamy texture and oak spice
rounds off this pairing.*

Eggplant Parmesan Stacks
Makes 4 stacks

2 medium sized eggplants, sliced ¼" thick
4 eggs
1 ½ cups Italian herb flavored panko
  bread crumbs
½ cup parmesan cheese, grated
SplenDishes House Blend
¼ cup vegetable oil
2 cups marinara sauce
12 slices fresh mozzarella
Fresh basil leaves
½ cup parmesan cheese, shredded

1. Place eggplant slices on baking sheet, season both
   sides generously with SplenDishes House Blend.
2. In a shallow bowl, combine panko bread
   crumbs and grated parmesan cheese. In
   another shallow bowl, beat the eggs.
3. Heat a fry pan on medium-high heat and
   drizzle a few tablespoons of vegetable oil.
4. Dredge each eggplant slice in egg, then into
   the panko mixture, coating both sides. Place
   in hot oil and brown on both sides, about 4
   minutes each side. Remove from pan and
   place on paper towel-lined baking sheet.
5. To assemble, spoon some marinara sauce in
   center of dinner plate. Place an eggplant slice
   down on sauce, then layer with a piece of fresh
   mozzarella, repeating so you end up with the 3rd
   eggplant slice on top.
6. Spoon marinara sauce over tops of each stack
   and sprinkle with shredded parmesan cheese.
7. Garnish with fresh basil and serve.

Chicken Piccata
Serves 4

4 chicken cutlets
SplenDishes House Blend
1 tablespoon olive oil
3 tablespoons butter
3 garlic cloves
2 lemons, 1 juiced and 1 thinly sliced for garnish
1 cup dry white wine
1 cup chicken stock
3 tablespoons capers
2 tablespoons flour plus 2 tablespoons
  melted butter
1 tablespoon flat-leaf parsley, chopped

1. Season chicken cutlets on both sides with
   SplenDishes House Blend.
2. Heat a sauté pan on medium high heat.
   Once pan is hot, add 2 tablespoons olive oil,
   then place chicken in pan. Cook on both
   sides until chicken is cooked through and
   golden brown, about 4-5 minutes on each
   side. Remove from pan and set aside.
3. In the same pan, lower heat slightly and add
   3 tablespoons butter and garlic. Sauté until
   lightly golden, then stir in the juice of one
   lemon, wine, and chicken broth. Bring to
   a boil, then lower heat and simmer for 10
   minutes (sauce will reduce by about half).
   Add capers and whisk in melted butter and
   flour mixture. Sauce will thicken quickly, then
   remove from heat.
4. To serve, place chicken on plates, spoon
   sauce over chicken, and garnish with parsley.

Want Wine?

Wine pairing suggestion:
Barbera

Wine notes for similiar choice:
*Very versatile wine. Delicious
with Italian syle dishes.*

Bacon Cheeseburger with Herbed Parmesan Truffle Fries
Makes 4 burgers

1 pound 80/20 ground beef
SplenDishes House Blend
8 slices thick cut applewood-smoked bacon
2 heirloom tomatoes, sliced
4 leaves butter lettuce
Blue cheese crumbles
Mayonnaise and mustard, if desired
4 knotted rolls, sliced in half
2 tablespoons butter, melted

1. Divide ground beef into 4. Using your hands, shape into 4 round patties, about 1-2 inches thick. Generously season each burger with House Blend. Cook the burgers until golden brown on each side, about 4 minutes each side. Burgers will be medium rare.
2. Brush both sides of knotted rolls with butter. Place on grill (or skillet) flat-side down until lightly golden (only brown the inside).
3. Assemble burgers with tomatoes, lettuce, bacon, and blue cheese, to your liking.

Herbed Parmesan Truffle Fries
½ bag frozen shoestring fries
½ cup grated parmesan cheese
2 tablespoons fresh rosemary and thyme, finely chopped
Pinch SplenDishes Bourbon Bacon Salt
White truffle oil, for drizzling

1. Preheat oven to 425° F.
2. Place baking sheet in oven and heat for 10 minutes.
3. Spread frozen fries in a single layer on hot baking sheet. Adjust oven heat and cook according to directions on bag.
4. Once done, place hot fries into a serving bowl. Toss with parmesan, herbs, and Bourbon Bacon Salt, then drizzle with truffle oil and toss again.

Crab Mac & Cheese
Serves 4-6

½ pound lump crab meat
2 tablespoons butter
4 ounces cream cheese
2 cups whole milk (or cream)
2 teaspoons SplenDishes House Blend
1-pound assorted cheeses, shredded
1-pound cooked pasta
Fresh parsley, chopped, for garnish

1. In a large sauce pan, melt butter and cream cheese, then whisk in 2 cups whole milk or cream. Continue whisking and stir in 2 teaspoons House Blend.
2. Fold in 1 pound of shredded cheese of your choice, and stir until melted and combined. Taste and re-season if needed.
3. Combine with 1 pound of cooked pasta. Add milk or cream if too thick and season with additional salt, if needed. Lastly, gently fold in crab meat, careful not to break up meat too much.
4. Garnish with chopped parsley.

Want Beer?

Beer pairing suggestion for Bacon Cheeseburger with Herbed Parmesan Truffle Fries:
India Pale Ale

Beer notes for similiar choice:
The hoppiness matches the intensity of the flavors.

Want Wine?

Wine pairing suggestion:
Chardonnay

Wine notes for similiar choice:
A creamy and buttery style will accentuate both flavor and texture of this dish.

Beer Batter-Fried Green Tomatoes with Bacon Aioli
Makes about 12 tomatoes

Bacon Aioli
3 pieces cooked bacon
½ cup mayonnaise
3 tablespoons lemon juice
1 garlic clove
Pinch of SplenDishes House Blend

Combine all ingredients in blender until creamy. Keep covered and refrigerated until ready to use.

Tomatoes
3 large green tomatoes, sliced to about ¼" thickness
⅔ cup corn meal
⅓ cup all-purpose flour
Pinch SplenDishes House Blend
Pinch cayenne pepper
½-¾ cup beer
Vegetable oil, for frying
SplenDishes Bourbon Bacon Salt, for finishing
Fresh parsley, chopped for garnish

1. Heat vegetable oil in large skillet. You only want about ½ inch of oil in the pan.
2. In a shallow bowl, combine corn meal, flour, House Blend and cayenne. Whisk in just enough beer, until a batter-like consistency forms (think pancake batter). Dip tomatoes into batter and carefully place into oil. Fry until golden brown, about 3-4 minutes each side.
3. Drain on paper towel and season with SplenDishes Bourbon Bacon Salt.
4. Place tomatoes on platter, garnish with parsley.
5. Serve hot alongside Bacon Aioli.

Want Beer?
Beer pairing suggestion for Beer-Batter-Fried Green Tomatoes with Bacon Aioli:
Pale Ale

Beer notes for similiar choice:
Slightly bitter beer that refreshes your palate.

Campfire Chicken
Serves 6

6 pieces chicken (any type you like, breasts, thighs, legs, etc.)
3 corn cobs, cut in half
1 pound baby red potatoes
1 red onion, roughly chopped
6 large carrots, cut into thirds
SplenDishes BBQ Rub
Kosher salt
2-3 dark beers

1. Using about a 12 inch square of heavy duty aluminum foil, place 1 piece of chicken, ½ corn cob, a few baby red potatoes, some onion, and carrots into center of foil. Season generously, with about ½ tablespoon of SplenDishes BBQ Rub and a pinch of salt.
2. Bring edges up leaving center open, making an open pouch. Place on baking sheet and continue with remaining 5 pouches.
3. Heat BBQ* on medium high heat and place pouches on grill. Fold top of foil to seal pouches. Pour about ½ beer (or so) into each pouch, so liquid is about ½ way covering chicken and veggies.
4. Close grill and cook for about 25 minutes or until chicken is cooked through (this depends on what type of chicken you used (bone-in will take longer). Be sure to check after about 15 minutes for level of liquid and add more if needed.
5. Remove from grill, place each pouch on serving plates, and serve as is.
6. Makes for a great presentation!

*This dish can also be done in the oven! Place in 400° F oven for about 30 minutes or until chicken is cooked through.

**Shrimp with Asparagus and Linguine
(Shaiyla's Favorite Pasta)**
Serves 4

1 pound 16-20 count Argentine pink shrimp,
  peeled and deveined
12 grape or cherry tomatoes, cut in half (optional)
½ pound asparagus, cut into 2" pieces,
  saving 8 sprigs for garnish
3 tablespoons applewood rub
3 tablespoons butter
1 tablespoon olive oil, plus extra for drizzling
Pinch of salt
½ cup dry white wine
½ pound linguine pasta, cooked according to
  directions on box
Flat leaf parsley, chopped for garnish

1. Preheat oven to 400° F.
2. Place asparagus pieces and 8 sprigs on baking
   sheet. Drizzle with olive oil and roast for 8
   minutes. Set aside.
3. Heat a skillet on medium-high heat. Add
   olive oil, shrimp, and tomatoes. Sprinkle with
   applewood rub and salt. Stir in wine and add
   butter. Bring to a boil, then lower heat and
   simmer for 5-6 minutes (this will cook the
   alcohol out).
4. Turn heat off and toss in roasted asparagus.
5. To serve, divide cooked linguine into
   4 shallow pasta bowls. Spoon shrimp,
   asparagus, and sauce over top of pasta and
   garnish each bowl with 2 asparagus sprigs and
   fresh parsley.

This is my daughter Shaiyla's favorite and most-requested dish. She loves the white wine and butter sauce. For a six-year-old, she has an amazing palate and often asks for lobster to go with her filet! She is the inspiration of so many things I do, and her love of cooking warms my heart.

Want Wine?

**Wine pairing suggestion
for Shimp with Asparagus
and Linguine**
Unoaked Chardonnay

Wine notes for similiar choice:
*Clean and crisp. Perfect match
with the sauce*

BLT Sandwich with Sundried Tomato Spread
Makes 2 sandwiches

Sundried Tomato Spread
4 ounces sundried tomatoes
¼ cup mayonnaise
Fresh cracked black pepper
Pinch of SplenDishes Bourbon Bacon Salt

Combine all ingredients in a small
food processor and pulse to combine.

Sandwich
4 thick-cut slices of your favorite bread,
  toasted on one side
1 large heirloom tomato, cut into 4 thick-cut slices
2 large pieces of butter lettuce
Fresh avocado, sliced
4 thick-cut slices of applewood smoked bacon

Assemble sandwich by generously spreading
the sundried tomato spread over both sides of
the toasted part of the bread. Then layer with
tomatoes, lettuce, avocado, and bacon.

This recipe originally came from my dad, or OD as I call him. It eventually morphed into my own, like so many others. Thanks, Dad, for the inspiration!

Game Day Chili
Serves 4-6

1 pound ground turkey
1 yellow onion, chopped
2 cloves garlic, chopped
1 tablespoon olive oil
2 cans dark red kidney beans
2 (14-ounce) cans fire-roasted tomatoes
3 tablespoons chili powder
1 tablespoons cumin
1 tablespoon SplenDishes House Blend
2 bottles of dark beer
  (can substitute 3 cups chicken stock)

1. Heat a large Dutch oven pot on medium-high heat. Add olive oil and sauté onions and garlic until tender, about 4 minutes. Stir in meat, breaking up with a spoon and cook about 5-6 minutes.
2. Add chili powder, cumin, and House Blend. Stir until combined.
3. Stir in kidney beans, tomatoes, and beer. Bring to a boil, then reduce heat and simmer on low for 45 minutes to an hour. Chili can also be transferred to a slow cooker, keep on low for about 4-6 hours.
4. Set up condiments in small bowls and let guests make their own.

Toppings
Cheddar cheese, shredded
Scallions (green onion), chopped
Pickled jalapenos
Sour cream (Greek yogurt is a great low-calorie substitute)

Sweet Buttery Bacon Cornbread
Serves 4-6

½ pound bacon, chopped
½ cup salted butter, melted
½ cup sugar
2 eggs
1 cup buttermilk (can be substituted with 1 cup milk plus 1 tablespoon vinegar)
1 can creamed corn
1 cup all-purpose flour
1 cup cornmeal
½ tsp baking soda
2 tablespoons brown sugar

1. Preheat oven to 375° F.
2. Heat a cast iron skillet on medium heat. Add bacon and slowly cook until the bacon fat renders and the bacon itself is slightly crispy. Remove from heat (leave the bacon fat in the pan).
2. While the bacon is cooking, combine melted butter, sugar, eggs, buttermilk, and creamed corn in a large bowl.
3. Stir in flour, cornmeal, and baking soda and mix until combined.
4. Pour batter into pan with cooked bacon. Sprinkle top with brown sugar and bake for 40-50 minutes or until toothpick inserted in center comes out clean.

Want Beer?

Beer pairing suggestion:
Amber Lager

Beer notes for similiar choice:
Let the Chili fill you up and enjoy the slight sweet malt to calm the spice.

Salmon with Butter and Dill
Serves 4

4 (6-ounce) salmon filets
SplenDishes House Blend
2 tablespoons olive oil
3 tablespoons butter, melted
1 tablespoon fresh dill, finely chopped,
  plus extra for garnish
1 lemon

1. Season salmon filets generously with House
   Blend. Combine melted butter and dill. Slice
   lemon in half. Using one of the halves, squeeze
   just a splash of juice into the butter mixture.
2. Heat skillet on medium high heat. Add olive
   oil, then place salmon skin-side up in the pan.
   Sear for 3-4 minutes, then flip over. Spoon
   butter mixture over tops of salmon, while it
   finishes cooking.
3. To serve, garnish with fresh lemon slices and
   dill sprigs.

Want Wine?

**Wine pairing suggestion for
Salmon with Butter and Dill:**
Pinot Noir

Wine notes for similiar choice:
*Excellent with Salmon and acid
that cuts the butter sauce.*

Savory Heirloom Tomato Pie
with Sour Cream Bacon Crust
Serves 6-8

Crust
2 ¼ cups self-rising flour
1 cup cold butter, cut up
6-8 bacon slices, cooked
⅔ cup sour cream

Filling
2 pounds large tomatoes (assorted colors and sizes)
1 teaspoon kosher salt
1 cup cheddar cheese, shredded
½ cup parmesan cheese, shredded
½ cup mayonnaise
1 egg, beaten
2 tablespoons fresh dill, chopped
1 tablespoon chives, chopped
1 tablespoon flat-leaf parsley, chopped
1 tablespoon apple cider vinegar
1 green onion, thinly sliced
2 teaspoons sugar
SplenDishes Bourbon Bacon Salt
1 tablespoon yellow cornmeal

To Make Crust
1. Using a food processor, pulse flour and cold
   butter until mixture resembles small peas.
2. Add bacon to flour/butter mixture; pulse just
   until combined. Add sour cream, and pulse
   until dough forms.
3. Spoon mixture onto a floured surface;
   sprinkle lightly with flour, and knead 3 or 4
   times, adding more flour as needed. Roll to
   a 13-inch round. Place dough in a 9-inch pie
   pan. Press dough into pan; trim off excess
   dough along edges. Chill 30 minutes.

To Make Filling
1. Slice tomatoes into ¼-inch thick slices, and
   remove seeds. Place tomatoes in a single
   layer on paper towels and sprinkle with 1
   teaspoon salt. Let stand about 10 minutes.
2. Preheat oven to 425° F.

3. In a large bowl, combine cheeses,
   mayonnaise, egg, herbs, apple cider vinegar,
   and sugar, until well combined.
4. Pat tomato slices dry with a paper towel.
   Sprinkle cornmeal over bottom of crust.
   Spread a thin layer of cheese mixture
   onto crust; layer with half of tomato slices
   in slightly overlapping rows. Top with ½
   cup cheese mixture. Repeat layers, using
   remaining tomato slices and cheese mixture
   (save 1 layer of tomatoes for top). Arrange
   remaining tomatoes on top of pie.
5. Bake at 425° F for 40 to 45 minutes,
   protecting edges with foil during last 20
   minutes to prevent excessive browning.
   Let stand 1 to 2 hours before serving.

Want Wine?

**Wine pairing suggestion for
Savory Heirloom Tomato Pie:**
Pinot Blanc

Wine notes for similiar choice:
*Citrus fruits with dryness and
acidic. Pairs well with tomato
and will have you ready for the
next bite.*

Turkey Meatloaf with Cauliflower Mash

Turkey Meatloaf
Serves 4

1 pound ground turkey
4 slices thick cut bacon, chopped
1 yellow onion, chopped
2 tablespoons olive oil
1 tablespoon SplenDishes House Blend
1 cup Homemade BBQ Sauce (see page 55 for recipe) (with Guinness Ribs)

1. Place skillet on medium-high heat. Add oil, bacon, and onions. Sauté until golden and caramelized, about 10 minutes. Remove from heat and let slightly cool.
2. Preheat oven to 375° F.
3. In a large bowl, add ground turkey, House Blend, and bacon mixture (including bacon fat).
4. Mix just until combined. Do not overmix, or the meatloaf will become tough after cooked.
5. Pour mixture out onto parchment-lined baking sheet. Form meat into a log-like shape, about 2 inches in height.
6. Slather generously with Homemade BBQ Sauce and bake for 20-25 minutes, or until inserted thermometer reads 160°F.

Cauliflower Mash
Makes about 1 ½-2 cups.

1 head of cauliflower
1 tablespoon butter, softened
4 ounces cream cheese, softened
1 teaspoon SplenDishes House Blend

1. Cut cauliflower into large chunks, leaving stalks on, then steam until fork tender. Place cauliflower into food processor with butter, cream cheese, and House Blend. Blend until creamy and well-combined.
2. Re-season to taste, if needed.

Want Wine?

Wine pairing suggestion:
Australian Shiraz

Wine notes for similiar choice:
Jammy style of wine to stand up to the bold flavors.

Perfectly Roasted Chicken

1 (5-pound) whole chicken
1 stick of salted butter, cut into thick slices
2 tablespoons bacon fat (vegetable oil or
 melted butter can be substituted)
3 tablespoons SplenDishes Bourbon Bacon Salt
2 onions, peeled and quartered
2 lemons, quartered
6 sprigs fresh rosemary
4 whole carrots
4 whole stalks celery
1 cup white wine
2 cups water

1. Preheat oven to 400° F.
2. Remove chicken from packaging, remove
 neck and innards, and discard. Pat chicken
 dry with paper towels.
3. Gently loosen skin from chicken breast, and
 around leg area. Arrange slices of butter
 under skin on breast and leg.
4. Fill cavity with a few of the onion and
 lemon quarters and rosemary sprigs, then
 tie the legs together with kitchen twine.
 Sprinkle the whole top and sides of chicken
 generously with Bourbon Bacon Salt.
5. In a large roasting pan, place carrots, celery
 and the remaining onions and lemon, making
 a bed for the chicken to lay on.
6. Place chicken on vegetables and pour wine
 and water into pan. Toss remaining rosemary
 along sides of chicken.
7. Place chicken in oven and roast for 1 ½ hours
 or until juices run clear.
8. Let chicken rest for 10 minutes before carving.

Want Wine?

**Wine pairing suggestion for
Perfectly Roasted Chicken:**
Beaujolais

Wine notes for similiar choice:
*Great fruit forward French red
that pairs well with chicken.*

Braised Short Ribs with Red Wine Sauce
Serves 4-6

3-4 pounds of beef short ribs
SplenDishes Bourbon Bacon Salt
2 tablespoons flour, plus 2 additional
 tablespoons for later
2 tablespoons vegetable oil
1 bag white pearl onions, peeled
2 garlic cloves
6 cherry tomatoes, cut in half
1 tablespoon vegetable bouillon paste
1 bottle dry red wine
2 fresh rosemary stems
2 tablespoons butter
1 small bunch of whole baby carrots, washed and
 stems cut off
1-pound baby Yukon potatoes
Olive oil, for drizzling
SplenDishes House Blend

1. Preheat oven to 350° F.
2. Heat a Dutch oven on high heat. Season short
 ribs generously with SplenDishes Bourbon
 Bacon Salt, then dust with flour. Add vegetable
 oil blend to hot pot and add meat. Brown on
 both sides for about 3-4 minutes, then remove
 from pan.

Want Wine?

**Wine pairing suggestion for
Perfectly Roasted Chicken:**
California Cabernet Sauvignon

Wine notes for similiar choice:
*Big, bold, rich cab to match the
the style of this dish.*

3. Add onions and garlic cloves and sauté about
 4 minutes. Stir in vegetable bouillon, then
 deglaze pan with red wine, scraping up all the
 brown bits from the bottom of the pan.
4. Place meat back in pan and place rosemary
 stems and tomato halves on top.
5. Tent pot with aluminum foil and braise in
 oven for 1 hour. Remove foil and continue
 braising for an additional 30-45 minutes.
 Check liquid level to make sure it's not too
 low, add more wine if needed.
6. Now, place potatoes and carrots on baking
 sheet. Drizzle with olive oil blend and sprinkle
 with SplenDishes House Blend. Place in rack
 below pot with beef. Toss once in between
 and cook until fork tender.
7. When beef and vegetables are done, remove
 from oven and let rest.
8. In a small bowl, combine 2 tablespoons
 melted butter and 2 tablespoons flour.
 Remove beef from pot and place on serving
 platter. Skim as much fat as possible from
 meat off the top of the remaining liquid
 and discard.
9. Whisk in butter/flour mixture and sauce
 will thicken. Taste and re-season with salt,
 if needed. Spoon sauce over beef and serve
 potatoes and carrots on side.

Grilled Tri-Tip Steak with Chimichurri Sauce
Serves 4

2 pound tri-tip steak
6 large cloves garlic, cut into halves
¼ cup soy sauce
¼ cup Worcestershire sauce
¼ cup balsamic vinegar
2 tablespoons Sriracha hot sauce
1 dark beer
1 tablespoon whole peppercorns
Fresh herb sprigs, such as rosemary, thyme, and/or oregano, plus extra for garnish
SplenDishes Bourbon Bacon Salt, for finishing

1. Place fat side of meat up on a board. Using a small sharp knife, pierce several slits deep into meat. Insert garlic pieces into slits.
2. In a large bowl (or ziplock bag), combine soy sauce, Worcestershire sauce, balsamic vinegar, Sriracha hot sauce, beer, and peppercorns. Place meat into bowl and submerse. Top with fresh herb sprigs, cover with plastic wrap, and refrigerate for 3-4 hours (can be done up to 24 hours before).
3. Heat grill on high. Place meat fat-side down and sear on both sides, about 4-5 minutes, each side. Adjust grill to indirect heat (outside 2 burners only) and grill on low heat for 25-30 minutes, basting in between. Internal temperature should register at 120° F for medium rare. Remove from grill and let rest for 10 minutes. Meat will continue to cook while resting and will reach 125° F. Slice meat against the grain and place on platter. Sprinkle with Bourbon Bacon Salt, and garnish with fresh rosemary sprigs.

Chicken Enchiladas with Homemade Verde Sauce
Serves 4

4 cups cooked and shredded chicken
2 cups fresh baby spinach
1 (14-ounce) can black beans, drained
24 ounces shredded pepper jack cheese
6 large flour tortillas
3 cups Verde Sauce (see recipe at right)

1. Preheat oven to 375° F.
2. Spoon 1 cup of the verde sauce in the bottom of a 9" x 13" baking dish.
3. To assemble enchiladas, spread about 4 ounces of chicken, 3 ounces spinach, and 2 tablespoons black beans onto each tortilla. Roll tortillas tightly, and place in baking dish.
4. Ladle remaining sauce over tops of enchiladas and cover with pepper jack cheese.
5. Bake for 20 minutes until cheese is golden and bubbling.

Homemade Verde Sauce
Makes approximately 3 cups

1 pound of tomatillos, leaves peeled
1 white onion
1 green bell pepper
2 jalapenos
4 cups water
3 cloves garlic
1 cup fresh cilantro
2 tablespoons dried oregano
1 teaspoon cumin
1 teaspoon salt, more if needed

1. Roughly chop tomatillos, onion, bell pepper, and jalapenos and toss in a large pot. Add water and bring to a boil. Lower heat and simmer for 20 minutes, until vegetables are tender. Add cilantro, then using an immersion blender, blend mixture in pot, until smooth.
2. Stir in cumin, dried oregano, and salt. Continue simmering for another 30 minutes. Sauce will reduce to about 3 cups.
3. Taste and add salt, if needed.

Want Beer?

Beer pairing suggestion for Grilled Tri-Tip Steak:
India Pale Ale

Beer notes for similiar choice:
The hoppiness matches the intense flavors and refreshes your palate.

My husband Eric, or the Grill Master as he is known on social media, is the king of the grill. From monster ribeyes, to smoked chicken, to this beautiful juicy tri-tip steak, he nails it every time. If you're a grill master in training, talk to Eric—he'll help you up your status!

Chimichurri Sauce

1 cup flat-leaf parsley
1 cup cilantro
6 large garlic cloves
¼ cup red wine vinegar
¾ - 1 cup extra-virgin olive oil
Pinch red pepper flakes
Pinch salt
Pinch cumin

1. Add all ingredients into a food processor and pulse until well-combined. Add more salt, if needed.
2. Keep refrigerated in sealed container for up to 10 days.

Fish en Papillote (in parchment)
Makes 2 servings

2 (6-ounce) filets of sea bass, halibut, or any
   light, flaky fish you like
8 ounces of greens (spinach, swiss chard),
   uncooked
1 fennel bulb, trimmed and sliced thinly
1 orange, sliced
Extra virgin olive oil, for drizzling
SplenDishes House Blend, for sprinkling
2 (14" x 14") pieces of parchment paper

1. Preheat oven to 450° F.
2. Place 2-3 slices of fennel just below the
   center of the parchment paper, then top
   with 4 ounces of the greens. Lightly sprinkle
   with SplenDishes House Blend, then top
   with fish. Drizzle generously with olive oil and
   season again with SplenDishes House Blend.
   Finish with a slice of orange.
3. Wrap parchment around fish tightly, folding
   edges to seal the fish in.
4. Place in oven and bake for 12 minutes until
   packets are puffed up and fish is cooked
   through. Let packets rest 3-5 minutes.
5. To serve, place each packet on serving plate
   and open!

Grilled Shrimp Tacos with Homemade Tortillas

Shrimp

1 pound 16-20-count shrimp, peeled
 and deveined
2 tablespoons SplenDishes BBQ Rub
½ teaspoon salt
3 tablespoons canola oil

1. In a bowl, whisk together canola oil, BBQ Rub, and salt. Toss with shrimp and marinate for 20 minutes. Heat grill on high heat. Place shrimp on grill and cook for 1 minute on each side. Remove from grill and serve.

Slaw

1 ½ cups shredded cabbage
1 tablespoon mayonnaise
1 tablespoon cider vinegar
1 teaspoon Sriracha hot sauce
Pinch SplenDishes House Blend

1. In a bowl, whisk together mayonnaise, vinegar, Sriracha hot sauce, and House Blend. Toss with cabbage and keep refrigerated until ready to use.

Tortillas

Makes approximately 16-20 tortillas

2 cups all-purpose flour (or whole wheat flour)
2 teaspoons baking powder
1 teaspoon salt
2 tablespoons vegetable shortening or lard
½ -¾ cup hot water

1. In a large bowl, combine dry ingredients then cut shortening in, blending until it looks like small peas. Stir in hot water until dough comes together, then knead about 30-40 times.
2. Cover with clean dish towel, and let dough rest for about 30 minutes.
3. Roll dough into the size of small golf balls, keeping in covered bowl.
4. Roll balls out to ⅛ inch thickness and place on baking sheet.
5. Heat flat skillet on high heat, place each tortilla in pan, and cook until bubbles start to form, about 30 seconds. Flip tortilla and cook another 20-30 seconds and place on covered plate.
6. Refrigerate extra tortillas in a sealed container for a week to 10 days.
7. Assemble tacos with your favorite accompaniments, such as chopped tomatoes, avocado, and cilantro.

Want Wine?

Wine pairing suggestion:
Pinot Gris

Wine notes for similiar choice:
Tropical fruits (melon) and low acid that will compliment the grilled shrimp.

Braised Turkey
Serves 4-6

2 turkey breasts, each cut into 2 pieces
2 turkey thighs
SplenDishes House Blend
⅓ cup vegetable oil
2 pieces thick-cut bacon, roughly chopped
1 onion, chopped
2 carrots, chopped
2 celery stalks, chopped
2 cloves garlic, chopped
1 tablespoon tomato paste
2 cups dry white wine
1 cup water
3 fresh cherry tomatoes, cut in half
2 sprigs each of fresh rosemary and thyme
2 tablespoons butter
Parsley, chopped, for garnish

1. Season turkey generously with SplenDishes House Blend.
2. Heat Dutch oven pot on high heat with vegetable oil. Brown turkey on both sides, about 5 minutes, and remove from pan.
3. Add bacon and cook 4-5 minutes, until lightly golden. Add a little more oil, then add onions, carrots, and celery and continue to sauté until onions are translucent, about 4-5 minutes. Season with SplenDishes House Blend, then stir in garlic and tomato paste. Continue stirring for additional 2-3 minutes, then add white wine. Scrape any browned bits from bottom of pan. Place turkey back into pot (if you're using skin-on turkey, place pieces skin-down) and pour in water. Liquid should only cover turkey ¾ up, so tops of meat are not submerged. Bring liquid to a boil over medium-high heat. Lay sprigs of rosemary and thyme and tomato halves on top and place in oven.
4. Tent with foil and braise for approximately 45 minutes, then turn turkey pieces over, and cook additional 30 minutes with foil removed, until turkey is fork tender. Once done, remove rosemary and thyme stems.
5. Remove turkey and place on platter. Spoon half the vegetables around the turkey. Using an immersion blender, blend the remaining vegetables and liquid until smooth. Stir in 2 tablespoons butter until melted and spoon sauce over turkey and vegetables.
6. Garnish with chopped parsley.

Want Wine?

Wine pairing suggestion:
Spanish Garnacha/Grenache

Wine notes for similiar choice:
Typically red fruits (raspberry, strawberry) with soft pepper finish. Light enough to not over power.

**Stuffed Pork Chops with Pan Gravy
and Roasted Brussels Sprouts**
Serves 4

4 (6-ounce) boneless, thick cut (center cut)
  pork chops
SplenDishes House Blend
1 shallot, chopped
2 garlic cloves, chopped
1 celery stalk, diced
4 tablespoons olive oil
2 tablespoons flat-leaf parsley, chopped
1 cup dry white wine
4 medium croissants, torn into small pieces
1 tablespoon butter or bacon fat
1 tablespoon all-purpose flour
1 cup beef stock (chicken stock can also be used)

1. Preheat oven to 375° F.
2. Heat a skillet on medium high heat. Add
   2 tablespoons of olive oil, shallots, garlic, celery,
   and a sprinkle of House Blend. Sauté until
   shallots are translucent, about 4-5 minutes. Stir
   in parsley and white wine. Bring to a boil, then
   lower heat and simmer for 5 minutes. Turn heat
   off and add croissant pieces, stirring until bread
   has absorbed all the liquid and mixture is well-
   combined. Taste and reseason, if needed.
3. Let mixture slightly cool.
4. Using a sharp knife, cut a pocket into the thickest
   part of the pork chop, then stuff each pork chop
   with stuffing. Season chops with House Blend.
5. Heat an ovenproof pan on medium-high heat.
   Add remaining 2 tablespoons olive oil and add
   pork. Brown on one side, about 4 minutes,
   then carefully flip chops over. Turn off heat and
   place in oven. Bake for 20-25 minutes or until
   pork is cooked through.
6. Once pork is done, remove chops from pan
   and let rest on plate.
7. Heat pan on medium and add butter and flour.
   Whisk until butter is melted and flour begins to
   turn lightly golden. Whisk in beef stock, scraping
   up any brown bits from bottom of pan. Bring to a
   boil and gravy will thicken. Season to taste.
8. Spoon over pork chops.

Brussels Sprouts
Serves 4

1 pound Brussels sprouts, quartered
Extra-virgin olive oil, for drizzling
SplenDishes Bourbon Bacon Salt
⅓ cup shredded parmesan cheese
⅓ cup dried cranberries
Balsamic syrup, for drizzling

1. Preheat oven to 375° F.
2. Place Brussels sprouts on baking sheet.
   Drizzle with olive oil and sprinkle with
   Bourbon Bacon Salt. Roast for 20-25
   minutes, tossing in between.
3. Transfer to serving platter. Sprinkle with
   parmesan cheese and cranberries, then
   drizzle with balsamic syrup.

Want Wine?

Wine pairing suggestion:
Rosé

Wine notes for similiar choice:
*Nothing goes with stuffing like
a Rosé.*

CHEF INSPIRED
RUSH ESPRESSO
CAFÉ & WINE BAR

Rush Espresso Café and Wine Bar is a favorite here in Charlotte. Locals love to stop in for amazing coffee, teas, and pastries, or grab something off their tasty lunch menu. Their dinner menu is even more delightful with an array of boutique-style wines and craft beers to choose from. Chef and owner, Paul McConachy, and his beautiful wife, Jennifer, have created three fantastic locations in Charlotte.

Chef Paul and I played in the kitchen, where he shared his prized recipe for authentic Australian Meat Pies. These pies have a rustic and rich meat sauce with a flaky, buttery pastry crust. They're wonderful paired with a lovely burgundy wine.

My love for wine is well-known! So, having a wine bar as one of my favorite places to hang out is ideal. It's even more ideal when you're friends with the bartender! My good friend, Stephen Johnson is the General Manager at Rush, as well as one of the bartenders and a sommelier. He always has my favorite glass of chardonnay ready for me and is the master when it comes to pairing food and wine. I was honored to have him pair all of the dishes in this book with wine or beer.

Try any one of Rush Espresso Café and Wine Bar's locations and you will be delighted with everything they have to offer.

Paul McConachy

Born in Australia and taking on an early passion for cooking and kitchen life, Paul started working in kitchens at 14 years of age and worked his way through school, sweating over the hot-side grills of busy Brisbane restaurants. A lengthy career in the Services after school strengthened his desire to return to the kitchen and café lifestyle.

After moving to the USA, the concept and vision of Rush Espresso Café & Wine Bar came to life, capturing European café culture for the Charlotte, North Carolina market. Paul's kitchens are founded on the freshest ingredients, crafted in-house and served in a contemporary atmosphere.

The successes of Rush Espresso Cafés have paved the way for a unique café-styled menu across breakfast, lunch, and dinner, refreshing in the American culinary scene.

Australian Meat Pie
Makes 24 pies

1 ½ pounds ground beef
2 pounds beef chuck, sliced and diced in
  small cubes
2 yellow onions, diced
3 cloves garlic, diced
3 cups ketchup
⅓ cup Worcestershire sauce
4 cups water
1 package brown gravy mix, mixed with 1 ½ cups
  water
1 tablespoon Vegemite® (optional)
2 tablespoons oregano, plus extra for sprinkling
  tops of pies
Salt and Pepper
12 sheets of puff pastry
24 aluminum pie shells
Cooking spray and all-purpose flour for dusting

1. Brown onions and ground beef (only),
   cooking off any fat liquid. Add ketchup,
   Worcestershire sauce, water, gravy mix,
   Vegemite, oregano, and cubed beef. Season
   with salt and pepper. Cook on low to medium
   heat for 30-45 minutes.

Pie Shell Prep
Grease and flour aluminum pie shells.
Cut puff pastry to size and insert into pie molds.
Insert wax paper and place medium coffee cup
  on top to hold form.
Bake at 350° F for 10-12 minutes.

1. Take cooled meat pie filling and pour 6
   ounces into prebaked base.
2. Cut a puff pastry top to size and lay over
   the top of pie mix, blending the edges of the
   shell and lid with prongs of a fork.
3. Brush with eggwash and sprinkle with oregano.
4. Bake for 15-20 minutes or until golden brown.
5. These pies can be frozen after baking. To
   reheat, thaw pies and bake at 350° F for 25
   minutes. Recipe can also be broken down into
   smaller amounts.

Stephen Johnson is the General Manager of Rush Espresso Café and Wine Bar. He has 20 years of restaurant experience and has received his Intro Sommelier certificate from the Court of Master Sommeliers. Born and raised in Richmond, VA he moved to Charlotte in 2006. His passion for wine was sparked by his mentor, Justin Boudrie, the General Manager at his first job in Charlotte. From there, Stephen went on to study wine and food pairings, working for Chef Paul Verica of Heritage Food and Drink before his start at Rush Espresso Café and Wine Bar.

CELEBRATIONS

Everyone loves a celebration. It could be a
holiday, birthday, anniversary, party, or even
a football game. Whatever you're celebrating,
great food is always a must! Here are some fun
and delicious ideas for you to try on one of your
special occasions.

Best Corned Beef, Ever

Once you've tried this recipe, you'll know why I named it the Best Corned Beef, Ever! For years I made my corned beef in the slow cooker, and don't get me wrong, it's tasty, but I always thought it could be better. I was flipping through a food mag one day about five years ago, and saw a test kitchen trying out different ways to make corned beef. One of the methods was topped with mustard, then wrapped in foil and baked in the oven. So, I tried it, and oh. my. delicious-ness! Of course, I tweaked it and made it mine. The meat is so juicy and tender, it's like butter. And the hearty stout mustard with brown sugar and crispy fat tips... yum. Try it once and you'll never make corned beef the old way again!

Best Corned Beef, Ever with Roasted Carrots & Potatoes and Sautéed Cabbage
Serves 4

2-3 pound corned beef brisket
8-10 whole cloves
¼ cup dark whole grain mustard
2 tablespoons brown sugar
6 yellow potatoes
6 carrots, peeled and cut in half
SplenDishes House Blend
SplenDishes Bourbon Bacon Salt
Olive oil
1 tablespoon flat-leaf parsley, chopped
1 tablespoon butter
1 head of cabbage, cored and thinly sliced
1 onion, chopped
2 garlic cloves, chopped
4-6 slices bacon, chopped

1. Preheat oven to 350° F.
2. Crisscross two pieces of heavy duty aluminum foil in a baking dish. Place corned beef fat-side up in the center of foil.
3. Pierce top of meat with cloves. Spread mustard over top, sprinkle with brown sugar, and fold foil to create a tightly sealed pouch. Bake for 2 hours.
4. After the first hour, place potatoes and carrots on baking sheet, drizzle with olive oil, sprinkle with SplenDishes Bourbon Bacon Salt, and bake until fork tender, about 45 minutes. Remove from oven, toss in a bowl with butter and parsley.
5. In a large pan, sauté bacon and onions until onions are opaque. Add sliced cabbage and cook until tender. Add garlic and 1 teaspoon of House Blend and continue to cook until cabbage, onions, and bacon start to caramelize, about 12-15 minutes. Season to taste.
6. Once meat is done, remove from foil pouch (discard the liquid) and place on baking sheet.
7. Switch oven to broil. Brush with a mustard and sprinkle with brown sugar. Broil meat until top is golden brown and bubbling, about 4-5 minutes.
8. Let meat rest for a few minutes, then slice against the grain and serve.

Football Sunday

Football is one of my guilty pleasures. If my team is playing, I'm sure to be home, watching with as few people as possible, occasionally screaming my way through the game. When it comes to the Big Game, there are endless ideas for dishes to make. I like to pick recipes that are easy to make ahead, so you aren't spending your time in the kitchen instead of watching your team. Enjoy the game and your guests!

Pimento Cheese Potato Boats
Makes 24 bite-sized pieces

1 cup pimento cheese
12 baby yellow potatoes
SplenDishes Bourbon Bacon Salt
4 slices thick cut bacon, cooked and crumbled

1. Cook potatoes in microwave or steam, until fork tender. Let slightly cool, then slice in half, length-wise. Score tops of potato (flesh side) with a fork, then sprinkle with SplenDishes Bourbon Bacon Salt.
2. Top each half with pimento cheese and crumbled bacon.
3. Place under broiler for 3-5 minutes until cheese is melted and bacon is crispy.

Buffalo Chicken Dip

2 (8-ounce) packages Cream Cheese, softened
1 cup ranch dressing
½ cup hot sauce
1 cup blue cheese crumbles
2 cup cheddar cheese, shredded
3 cups chicken, shredded
Tortilla chips or toasted baguette
Celery sticks

1. Preheat oven to 350° F.
2. In a large bowl, mix together softened cream cheese (microwave if needed), ranch dressing, hot sauce, blue cheese crumbles, cheddar cheese, and chicken.
3. Transfer to casserole dish and bake for about 15-20 minutes, until bubbling around edges. You could also transfer to a slow cooker and heat on low until bubbling, (turn down to warm setting once ready to serve).
4. Serve with tortilla chips, toasted baguette, and celery sticks.

Bacon Marmalade Dip

4 ounces SplenDishes Bacon Marmalade
1 tablespoon Sriracha hot sauce
1 cup cheddar cheese, shredded
1 cup monterey jack cheese, shredded
1 cup sour cream
1 cup mayonnaise
1 teaspoon SplenDishes House Blend
2 large Granny Smith apples, sliced and cored
1 baguette, sliced and toasted
Tortilla chips

1. Preheat oven to 400° F.
2. In a large bowl combine sour cream, mayonnaise, Sriracha hot sauce and SplenDishes House Blend. Stir in cheeses to combine, then fold in SplenDishes Bacon Marmalade.
3. Pour into ramekin or cast-iron pan and bake 20 minutes, or until golden and bubbling.
4. Serve hot with sliced Granny Smith apples, toasted baguette, and tortilla chips.

Want Beer?

Beer pairing suggestion:
India Pale Ale

Beer notes for similiar choice:
The citrus of the hops and sweetness of the malts will balance the heat.

Want Wine?

Wine pairing suggestion:
Marsanne-Roussane Blend

Wine notes for similiar choice:
French white wine blend that is made for turkey.

Turkey with Gravy

15-18 pound turkey, thawed
1 yellow onion, quartered
1 lemon, quartered
1 stick of butter, cut into ⅛" slices
¼ cup mixed fresh herbs, finely chopped
  (rosemary, thyme, and sage are great to use)
1 clove garlic, finely chopped
2 cups water
½ cup reserved bacon fat, chilled
2 ounces SplenDishes House Blend

Gravy

2 heaping tablespoons all-purpose flour
2 cups milk
Drippings from turkey pan, fat skimmed off
Salt and pepper, to taste

1. Preheat oven to 425° F.
2. Remove turkey from packaging, pull out bag of gizzards (sometimes its hidden in the neck area), and pat dry. Place on a rack in a large roasting pan.
3. Insert onion and lemon quarters into cavity. Gently separate skin from turkey breast and legs, leaving it still intact around edges.
4. In a small bowl, combine herbs and garlic and rub under the skin on breast and legs. Place pats of butter 1-2 inches apart under skin. Using a silicon band or kitchen twine, secure legs together.
5. Generously brush tops and sides of turkey with bacon fat, then coat with SplenDishes House Blend.

Thanksgiving

If you've been to one of my Thanksgivings, you know I take this holiday seriously. I look forward to the Fall season every year and get so excited for my favorite holiday. I've lived away from my family for over 15 years now, so every year, I throw a fabulous pre-Thanksgiving celebration for the friends I call family. It started with my friend Wendy in 2003. We invited eight friends and every year it grew and grew to sometimes over 30! I plan a month ahead and start cooking three days before. I don't let anyone bring anything but a nice bottle of wine. The sides are always pretty traditional (with a little spin on them), with the exception of one new secret side dish, which everyone tries to guess!

There are always two 20+ pound turkeys, but turkey #1 is always the star of the show. My signature turkey has this amazing glaze with roasted red peppers, jalapenos, and red currant jelly that keeps everyone wanting more. The glaze becomes part of the gravy, which makes you want to drink it with a straw! I hope you'll try this just once for your special Thanksgiving so you can see what the fuss is all about!

6. Add 2 cups water to bottom of pan and roast turkey at 425° F for 30 minutes. Reduce heat and continue roasting until turkey is cooked through and juices run clear.
7. Cooking times will vary, depending on the size of turkey, but it's usually 12-15 minutes per pound. Be sure to check the temperature regularly during roasting times.
8. The last hour of cooking, baste the turkey with glaze every 20 minutes until done.
9. Remove from oven and let rest for 15 minutes. Then, remove turkey from roasting rack, place on large platter, and continue to let rest for up to an hour before carving.
10. Skim as much fat as possible from drippings in the pan and discard. If your roasting pan fits on a stove burner (or 2), place on medium heat and sprinkle in flour. Whisk together with drippings and let flour cook for 2-3 minutes, then whisk in milk. Gravy will start to thicken as it comes to a boil. Season with salt and pepper to taste.
11. Transfer to a gravy boat and serve.

Chef's Gravy Tip: The 2-2-2 rule is a fool-proof way to always make the perfect gravy! The key is to use the same measurements for fat, flour, and liquid ratios. So, 2 tablespoons bacon fat, butter, or drippings, 2 tablespoons flour, and 2 cups milk or stock. This will make about 2 cups of gravy.

Turkey Glaze

2 cloves garlic
2 shallots, roughly chopped
8 slices pickled jalapeno
1 cup roasted red peppers
1 ½ cups dry white wine
1 small jar red currant jelly
  (can also use dark cherry jelly)
1 tablespoon olive oil

1. In a food processor, add garlic, shallots, jalapenos and red peppers. Pulse until ingredients are slightly minced.
2. Heat a sauce pan on medium high heat, add oil and pepper mixture and sauté until shallots are translucent, about 4-5 minutes.
3. Add red currant jelly and combine until melted, then stir in white wine. Bring to a boil, then lower heat and simmer for about 10-15 minutes, until sauce is slightly reduced and thickened.
4. Set aside and cover until ready to use. Can also be refrigerated until ready to be used.
5. The last hour of the turkey roasting, baste every 20 minutes with glaze. This is will become part of the drippings and will make an amazing gravy!

Tapas Party

A trip to Spain is on my bucket list. The food and wine there is one-of-a-kind. Some people like to bar-hop, I want to Tapas bar-hop! A "tapa," in Spanish cuisine, is an appetizer or snack. Right up my alley. I could live on tapas and wine (and bacon)!

A Tapas Party is fun to throw; there are so many selections and ideas to create. And always be sure to include some decadent cheeses, charcuterie, olives, nuts, and crusty breads with top-quality extra virgin olive oil for dipping.

Here are a few ideas from parties my business partner, Su and I have created. Su's Spanish Tortilla is one of the stars of this show!

Chorizo in Red Wine

1 pound Spanish cured chorizo,
 sliced on the diagonal
2 cups dry red wine
3 tablespoons dark honey
4 sprigs fresh rosemary, plus extra for garnish
Toothpicks for serving

1. Heat a large cast iron pan on medium-high heat. Add sliced chorizo into pan and sauté until slightly golden. Add red wine, honey, and rosemary. Lower heat and simmer for 15-20 minutes, until wine reduces, stirring frequently.
2. Remove from heat, toss in remaining rosemary sprigs, and serve in same pan with toothpicks.

Stuffed Peppers
Makes 12 peppers

6 mini sweet bell peppers,
 cut in halves and seeds removed
8 ounces goat cheese
½ teaspoon garlic paste
1 tablespoon fresh parsley, finely diced

1. Preheat oven to 400° F.
2. Place pepper halves on baking sheet and bake for 10-15 minutes, until softened and fork tender.
3. Fill each pepper with cheese mixture and place back on baking sheet. Switch oven to broil and place under broiler for 3-5 minutes, until cheese is slightly golden and bubbling.

Want Wine?

Wine pairing suggestion:
Rioja Crianza

Wine notes for similiar choice:
Spanish red normally made with mainly Tempranillo. Great with sausage and the earth notes goes well with the peppers.

Spanish Tortilla with Potatoes and Onions

½ cup olive oil
1 onion, thinly sliced
3 garlic cloves, crushed
2 medium potatoes, peeled and thinly sliced
8 eggs
Salt and pepper, to season

1. Pour oil into a small non-stick frying pan over a medium heat, then add the onion and potatoes.
2. Turn the heat down to low and cook for 25 to 30 minutes, or until the onions are turning golden and the potato slices are cooked through. Continue to stir gently to avoid breaking the potatoes apart.
3. Crack eggs into a mixing bowl, season with crushed garlic, salt, and black pepper, then whisk together with a fork.
4. When the onions and potatoes are cooked, remove the pan from the heat and carefully add them into the eggs. Transfer the mixture back into the frying pan and place it over a low heat. Cook for around 20 minutes, or until there's almost no runny egg on top.
5. Use a spatula to slightly lift and loosen the sides of the tortilla. Carefully flip the pan over a dinner plate to release the tortilla, then then slide it back into the pan and cook on the other side for another 5 to 7 minutes, or until golden and cooked through.
7. Turn out the tortilla onto a serving plate and then cut into wedges or squares. This dish can be served hot or cold and is great with Romesco Sauce!

Recipe shared by Su Kelley.

Want Wine?

Wine pairing suggestion:
Riesling

Wine notes for similiar choice:
The sweetness helps offset any spice.

Chicken Curry
Serves 4

1 whole chicken, cut into 8 pieces
3 tablespoons vegetable oil
2 small red chili peppers
1 teaspoon cumin
1 teaspoon coriander seed, ground
1 teaspoon turmeric
1 bay leaf
1 cinnamon stick
1 teaspoon sea salt
1 yellow onion, chopped
3 yellow potatoes, peeled and quartered
2 cups water

1. In a large pot, heat oil on medium-high heat and brown chicken on all sides, then remove and set aside. Reduce heat and add onions (and more oil, if needed) and sauté until translucent, about 3-4 minutes. Stir in cumin, coriander, turmeric, bay leaf, and cinnamon stick. Combine with onions and roasting spices for approximately 3-4 minutes. The longer you roast your spices, the darker your curry will be, be careful not to burn them. Break chilis up and add along with salt.
2. Add chicken, along with accumulated juices, back into pan. Coat chicken with onion and spices, then add water and potatoes.
3. Bring to a boil, then reduce heat and simmer, covered, for about an hour or until potatoes are fork tender.
4. Serve with steamed basmati rice and curried vegetables.

Puri
Makes about 40 puris

Puris are a puffy, whole wheat, deep-fried bread that is usually made on special occasions or for entertaining. Used to scoop up curries and vegetables.

4 cups whole wheat flour
½ teaspoon sea salt
¾ cup vegetable shortening
2 cups water
2 cups vegetable oil, for frying

1. Mix together flour, salt, and shortening, using a pastry cutter (or your fingers), cutting shortening into pea-size pieces.
2. Add water, starting with 1 cup, incorporating with a fork, then using hands to bring dough together. Dough should be the consistency of a pie dough. Add more water if needed to get correct consistency. Once dough comes together, knead for 5 minutes. Dough should be smooth and not stick to your hands (humidity and altitude will determine consistency).
3. Unlike most pastry doughs, this dough gets better the longer you knead it. Place dough back into bowl and cover with clean towel for about 15 minutes.

Curried Vegetables
Serves 4

1 head cauliflower, cut into large florets
2 zucchinis, sliced into ¼" slices
1 yellow onion, chopped
2 garlic cloves, chopped
1 teaspoon SplenDishes Garam Masala
1 teaspoon turmeric
1 teaspoon sea salt
2 tablespoons olive oil
½ cup water

4. After dough has rested, punch down and re-knead.
5. Pinch off walnut-sized pieces of dough and roll with hands into smooth balls, then place back into covered bowl.
6. Once all the balls have been formed, you are ready to roll out each puri with a rolling pin.
7. One ball at a time, quickly re-roll with hands, then flatten on board with fingers.
8. Using a rolling pin, roll each puri out evenly into a circle. Thickness should be like a tortilla.
9. If your dough is too sticky, you may need to flour your board and rolling pin. If you do not need flour, then you have achieved the right consistency.
10. Place each rolled out puri on baking sheet, making sure they do not touch.
11. Heat vegetable oil in deep pan, such as a wok (you want at least 2 inches of oil to fry in), bringing oil temperature to 365-375° F.
12. Place each puri, one at a time, in the oil, dabbing once or twice with the back of a slotted spoon, about 6-7 seconds, then flip puri over and repeat for another 4-5 seconds.
13. Drain puri in slotted spoon over oil, then place on paper towels to drain excess oil.

1. In a large sauté pan, add oil, onions, and garlic. Sauté until onions are translucent, about 3-4 minutes, then stir in turmeric, SplenDishes Garam Masala and salt. Roast spices for 3-4 minutes, then add cauliflower and zucchini, coating with spice mixture.
2. Add water, cover, and cook until cauliflower is tender, about 30 minutes.

I grew up eating the Indian food my mom and didima (grandmother) cooked for us, so these dishes are family recipes. Between my mom, didima, sister, brother, and me, we all have our own variations on these dishes. However, they all come from the same place—our heart.

Indian food is a labor of love. It takes most of the day to make a feast, but in the end, it's well worth it.

I don't make it very often, so when I do, I go all out! I hope you enjoy my family's dishes and share them with your family.

Guinness® Ribs with Bacon Potato Salad and Strawberry Pretzel Salad

Any pit master will tell me this is not the traditional way to make BBQ, but I beg to differ. (And after you've had these Guinness Ribs, you might agree!) These ribs have won several awards and even won me my first fancy KitchenAid® mixer! How do you go wrong with savory pork ribs, simmered in beer, and topped with homemade BBQ sauce?

My Bacon Potato Salad has become kind of famous, and it's probably the most popular and requested side dish I make. I serve it at the same wine event every month, and people come just for this salad. (Ok, they come for the wine and music, too!) It's a great side dish for any occasion and is perfect served warm or at room temperature.

I'm relatively new to the South, so I had never heard of a Strawberry Pretzel "Salad," and even when a friend presented it to me, I was skeptical...that is, until I took a bite. I couldn't stop eating it. If you're a sweet and savory combo type of person, this salad will quickly become your favorite. It's a complex juxtaposition of flavors and textures: umami, sweet, salty, creamy, crunchy, and oh so heavenly.

Whip up this spread of dishes for your next cookout and treat your family and friends to a little piece of heaven!

Want Beer?

Beer pairing suggestion:
Milk Stout

Beer notes for similiar choice:
Roasted malts help accentuate the deeper flavors while the sweet notes ties this pairing together.

Guinness Ribs
Serves 4-6

2 racks pork ribs
2 Guinness beers
2 cups water
3 tablespoons SplenDishes BBQ Rub
2 cups homemade BBQ Sauce

1. Place ribs in large stovetop pan, add beer and water.
2. Cover loosely with aluminum foil and simmer on medium-low for about 1 to 1 ½ hours. Meat will be very tender.
3. Once done, remove from heat and discard liquid. Season both sides of meat carefully, with SplenDishes BBQ Rub and set aside until ready to grill, keeping covered.
4. Heat grill on high. Place ribs on a baking sheet and baste with homemade BBQ Sauce.
5. Place ribs on grill, basting a couple of times with BBQ Sauce until sauce caramelizes, approximately 8-10 minutes each side.

Homemade BBQ Sauce
Makes about 2 cups

1 shallot, finely chopped
2 garlic cloves, finely chopped
1 tablespoon canola oil
2 cups ketchup
⅓ cup brown sugar
⅓ cup molasses
¼ cup apple cider vinegar
½ cup Guinness Stout beer
1 tablespoon Worcestershire sauce
1 tablespoon Sriracha hot sauce
1 teaspoon SplenDishes House Blend

1. Heat a large sauce pan on medium heat, add oil, shallots, and garlic. Sauté until shallots are translucent, about 3-4 minutes. Whisk in remaining ingredients and bring to a low boil. Lower heat and simmer for 30-40 minutes, stirring occasionally, until sauce reduces and thickens.

Strawberry Pretzel Salad
Serves 8-10

Crust
2 ½ cups crushed pretzels
¾ cup butter, melted
3 tablespoons brown sugar

Mix together and press into a 9" x 13" baking dish. Bake at 400° F for 10 minutes. Let cool.

Filling
8 ounces cream cheese, softened
1 cup granulated white sugar
1 (8-ounce) container of Cool Whip®, thawed

Combine cream cheese and sugar, then fold in Cool Whip. Spread over cooled pretzel crust and keep refrigerated.

Topping
6 ounces strawberry Jell-O®
2 cups boiling water
20 ounces strawberries, sliced

1. Mix together strawberry Jell-O with boiling water. Stir in strawberries, then let sit until it starts to set up slightly. Then pour onto whipped topping and place in fridge to set.

2. Let chill for about 2 hours before serving.

Bacon Potato Salad
Serves approximately 4-6

1 pound of potatoes, cut into quarters
1 ear of corn
1 tablespoon SplenDishes House Blend
Pinch of red pepper flakes
4 slices bacon, chopped
1 sweet yellow onion, finely chopped
1 teaspoon fresh rosemary, chopped
1 tablespoon flat-leaf parsley, chopped, plus extra for garnish
½ pound cherry tomatoes, cut in halves
⅓ cup apple cider vinegar
2 tablespoons fresh lemon juice
¼ cup extra-virgin olive oil
SplenDishes Bourbon Bacon Salt

1. Preheat oven to 400° F.
2. Place potatoes and corn on baking sheet. Drizzle potatoes with olive oil and sprinkle with House Blend and red pepper flakes. Brush corn with olive oil and season the same. Roast in oven for 20-25 minutes, tossing in between, until potatoes are golden brown and fork tender.
3. To make the dressing, heat a skillet on medium heat. Add bacon and onions and slowly cook until onions and bacon start to turn light golden and caramelized, about 8-10 minutes. Keep bacon fat in pan and stir in tomatoes and rosemary. Continue cooking until tomatoes soften and start to release their juices, about 5 minutes.
4. Add cider vinegar and lemon juice and turn heat off. Drizzle in olive oil and mix well.
5. Remove corn kernels with a sharp knife and add to a large mixing bowl, along with the potatoes.
6. Stir in dressing and mix well.
7. Garnish with fresh, chopped parsley.
8. Salad can be served warm or at room temperature.

French Toast with Praline Pecan Syrup
Serves 2

Syrup
1 cup firmly-packed brown sugar
⅓ cup butter, plus extra for browning the French toast
2 tablespoons maple syrup
¾ cup pecans, chopped
Pinch SplenDishes Bourbon Bacon Salt

French Toast
½ French bread loaf (approximately four
  1½ inch thick slices)
4 eggs, beaten
1 cup milk
2 tablespoons sugar
1 teaspoon SplenDishes Pumpkin Pie Blend
1 teaspoon vanilla extract

1. Slice French bread into 1 inch slices.
2. Whisk together eggs, milk, sugar, SplenDishes
   Pumpkin Pie Blend, and vanilla. Soak bread
   slices in mixture for 30-60 minutes.
3. In a small sauce pan, melt butter and brown
   sugar. Add maple syrup and pecans. Bring to a
   boil, then lower heat and simmer for about 5-8
   minutes. Set aside until ready to use. Excess
   can be stored in sealed container in refrigerator
   for up to 10 days.
4. Heat a fry or sauté pan on medium-high heat,
   add butter until melted.
5. Carefully remove soaked bread, draining excess
   egg mixture off, and place into pan. Brown
   on both sides, until golden brown, about 3-4
   minutes on each side.
6. Serve immediately with warmed syrup.

Want Wine?

Wine pairing suggestion:
Port

Wine notes for similiar choice:
*Nutty and caramel flavors works
beautifully with this dish.*

Pork 4 Ways

Anytime I can take one piece of meat and make it into four different meals, I call that a win. These ideas are perfect for a celebration, where you can make a "Pulled Pork Bar" and give your guests options to make sliders, tacos, and nachos. Its also a great way to plan your weeknight meals or meal prep.

Pulled Pork

5-7-pound pork shoulder, center-cut butt
2 ounces SplenDishes BBQ Rub
  SplenDishes Bourbon Bacon Salt, to taste

1. Place pork fat-side up in a slow cooker. Coat meat generously with SplenDishes BBQ Rub. Cover and cook on low for 8 hours.
2. Once pork is done, remove from slow cooker, place on baking sheet, and let cool. Reserve liquid to use once meat is shredded. Once pork is cool enough to touch, shred meat using 2 forks. Season to taste with SplenDishes Bourbon Bacon Salt and BBQ Rub. Add enough cooking juices back into meat, just until moist. Keep meat covered and refrigerated until ready to use.

BBQ Pulled Pork Sliders
Makes 8 sliders

1 pound prepared Pulled Pork
½ cup Homemade BBQ Sauce
  (see page 55 for recipe)
16 bread and butter pickle slices
Homemade slaw
8 slider buns

Homemade Slaw

2 cups shredded cabbage
½ cup mayonnaise
3 tablespoons apple cider vinegar
1 teaspoon Sriracha hot sauce
½ teaspoon SplenDishes House Blend

1. Whisk together mayonnaise, vinegar, Sriracha
   hot sauce and SplenDishes House Blend.
   Fold in cabbage and mix well. Chill until ready
   to use.
2. To assemble sliders, place about 2 ounces of
   pork on each bun, drizzle with Homemade
   BBQ Sauce, then top with pickles and
   Homemade Slaw.

Want Wine?

Wine pairing suggestion:
American Sauvignon Blanc

Wine notes for similiar choice:
*Lime and Lemon notes and acid
flatters all 4 offerings.*

Skillet Nachos

1 pound prepared Pulled Pork
1 bag tortilla chips
8 ounces cheddar cheese, shredded
8 ounces monterey jack cheese, shredded
8 ounces Cotija Mexican cheese
1 can seasoned black beans, drained
1 cup Homemade BBQ Sauce (see page 55
  for recipe)
1 cup fresh-chopped tomatoes
2 avocados, cubed
1 jalapeno, thinly sliced
Fresh cilantro
Sour cream, optional

1. Preheat oven to 350° F.
2. Using a 13 inch cast iron skillet, begin layering ingredients, starting with tortilla chips, cheeses, black beans, and a drizzle of BBQ sauce. Repeat layer at least once, and depending on the depth of your skillet, repeat with a third layer, ending with a layer of cheese.
3. Place in oven for 10-12 minutes or until cheese is melted and bubbling. Remove from oven, drizzle with BBQ Sauce, then top with fresh tomatoes, avocado, jalapeno, and cilantro.
4. Serve in hot skillet and be sure to warn your guests of the hot pan!

Pulled Pork Tacos

1 pound prepared Pulled Pork
Homemade Slaw (see page 55 for recipe)
Fresh chopped tomatoes, avocado, cilantro
Limes
Homemade Tortillas (see page 37 for recipe)

To assemble tacos, place 2 ounces of pork on each tortilla, top with Homemade Slaw, fresh tomatoes, avocado, and cilantro. Garnish with fresh lime slices.

Pork Chili Verde
Serves 4

2 pounds prepared Pulled Pork
2 cups Homemade Verde Sauce
 (see page 34 for recipe)
Radishes, thinly sliced
Cilantro for garnish
Homemade Tortillas (see page 37 for recipe)

1. In a small Dutch oven, simmer pork with
   Homemade Verde Sauce for 20 minutes.
2. Top with sliced radishes, fresh cilantro, and
   serve with Homemade Tortillas.

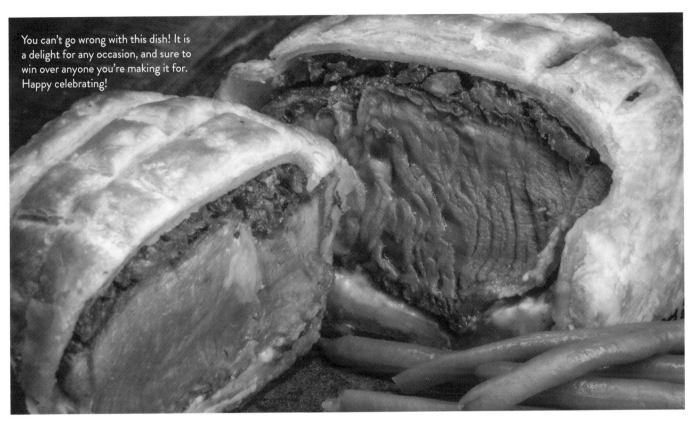

You can't go wrong with this dish! It is a delight for any occasion, and sure to win over anyone you're making it for. Happy celebrating!

Beef Wellington
Serves 2

2 (8 ounce) filet mignon steaks, about 2" thick
1 tablespoon SplenDishes House Blend
3 tablespoons butter
2 slices thinly-sliced prosciutto
4 ounces sundried tomatoes
6 large basil leaves
1 tablespoon extra-virgin olive oil
Pinch of salt and black pepper
1 sheet puff pastry, chilled
1 egg, beaten
Pinch of SplenDishes Bourbon Bacon Salt

1. Generously season both sides of steaks with SplenDishes House Blend. Heat a cast iron pan on medium-high heat. Once pan is hot, add butter and steaks. Sear steaks for about 3 minutes on each side. Remove from pan, place on a plate and immediately refrigerate. Chill for 1 hour.
2. In a small food processor, combine sundried tomatoes, basil, olive oil, salt, and pepper. Pulse until well combined.
3. Preheat oven to 425° F.
4. Lay puff pastry sheet out on lightly-floured board. Using a rolling pin, just slightly roll dough out, then cut in half. Spread half of the sundried tomato mixture in the center of pastry, then place prosciutto over mixture. Place chilled filet in center and fold pastry over meat, tucking sides underneath. Steak should be sealed in pastry. Repeat with second filet.
5. Place on parchment-lined baking sheet, brush tops and sides with egg, and sprinkle with SplenDishes Bourbon Bacon Salt. Bake for 20-25 minutes, or until pastry is golden brown and puffy. Meat will be medium rare.
4. Serve with your favorite vegetable.

Want Wine?

Wine pairing suggestion:
Bordeaux

Wine notes for similiar choice:
French red blend mainly Cabernet Sauvignon, Merlot, and Cab Franc. This full bodied red holds up to any flavorful dish.

If you're feeling indulgent, then make this dish for a loved one. They will love you forever! You will definitely have leftover crab, so be sure to make extra hollandaise sauce and save it for a scrumptious eggs benedict topped with crab, or pour it over your favorite veggies, like steamed broccoli, cauliflower, or asparagus.

Steak Oscar
Serves 2

2 (8 ounce) filet mignon steaks, about 2" thick
SplenDishes Bourbon Bacon Salt
1 tablespoon butter
1 tablespoon olive oil
4 spears of asparagus, trimmed and blanched*
4 ounces jumbo lump crab meat
Hollandaise Sauce

1. Preheat oven to 450° F.
2. Season meat generously with Bourbon Bacon Salt. Heat an ovenproof skillet on medium-high heat. Add butter and olive oil.
3. Add steaks and sear on both sides until golden brown crust forms, about 1 ½ minutes each side. Place skillet in oven to finish cooking steaks. Cook until medium rare, about 4-5 minutes.
4. Remove from oven and let steaks rest for 5 minutes.
5. To serve, place each steak on serving plate and place 2 spears of asparagus on top. Place 3-4 pieces of lump crab on top and drizzle with hollandaise sauce.

*To blanch asparagus, drop spears into boiling water for 2-3 minutes. Remove from pot and place in ice-cold water to stop cooking.

Hollandaise Sauce
Makes about ¾ cup

3 egg yolks
2 tablespoons lemon juice
2 sticks butter, melted
Pinch of salt
Pinch of cayenne pepper

1. In a blender or food processor, add egg yolks and blend. Add lemon juice and blend again until smooth. With the blender on, slowly drizzle in melted butter. Turn blender off and add salt and cayenne, and blend until thick and creamy. Set aside until ready to use. Keep extra sauce refrigerated in a sealed container for 2-3 days.

Want Wine?

Wine pairing suggestion:
Syrah

Wine notes for similiar choice:
Dark fruits that work well with grilling steaks: not too acidic or tannic to overpower the crab or sauce.

Want Wine?

Wine pairing suggestion:
Late Harvest Riesling

Wine notes for similiar choice:
A wine made from grapes left on the vine longer than normal. Crisp with a sweet finish.

Eggnog Bread Pudding with Maple Bacon Dust
Serves 6-8

4 slices maple-cured bacon
3 cups eggnog
⅓ cup sugar
3 eggs, beaten
1 loaf cinnamon swirl bread, torn into small pieces

1. Preheat oven to 375° F.
2. Place bacon slices on parchment paper-lined baking sheet. Bake for 15-18 minutes until crispy. Let cool, then place in food processor and pulse until crumbled. Spread crumbles on paper towel to dry and set aside.
3. Lower oven heat to 350° F.
4. In a large bowl, combine eggs, sugar, and eggnog. Fold in bread and let soak 10 minutes.
5. Place in greased 9" x 11" baking dish. Bake for 50-60 minutes, until center doesn't jiggle and top is golden and puffy.
6. Sprinkle bacon crumbles over top and serve.

Want Wine?

Wine pairing suggestion for Holiday Spice Cake:
Demi Sec Sparkling

Wine notes for similiar choice:
Bubbles with spicy tones to enhance the flavors.

Holiday Spice Cake

Cake
6 eggs
⅔ cup oil
1 cup canned pumpkin pie mix
⅔ cup water
2 tablespoons SplenDishes Pumpkin Pie Blend
1 box moist spice cake mix
1 box moist yellow cake mix

1. Preheat the oven to 350° F.
2. Butter and flour a 12-cup Bundt cake pan. In a large mixing bowl, combine the eggs, oil, pie mix, water, and pumpkin pie spice. Beat until well-blended. Add the cake mixes and stir to combine. Transfer the mixture to the prepared pan and bake for 50 minutes, or until a skewer inserted in the center comes out clean. Invert the cake onto a cooling rack.

Glaze
Red food coloring
1 (pound) bag of powdered sugar
⅓ cup orange juice, no pulp

1. Whisk the powdered sugar, orange juice, and red food coloring in a bowl, until well-combined. If the glaze seems too dry, add more water or orange juice to reach the right consistency. Drizzle the glaze over the cake.
2. Garnish with holiday items, such as holly stems and cranberries.

Recipe shared by Andi Gonzalez

I don't make a lot of cakes, but this one I make a few times every year, for different holidays. My friend Andi shared the recipe with me years ago when I saw the masterpiece she'd made for a fall celebration. I mostly make it for Christmas celebrations, because I love the bright red icing with the dark green holly branches; it makes for such a beautiful presentation. You can easily change this up for each holiday by changing the color of the icing and center piece decorations. Thank you, Andi, for sharing this. It will definitely be one of those recipes that gets passed on!

Strawberry Shortcake
Makes approximately 12-15 small shortcakes

2 cups strawberries
1-2 tablespoons sugar, optional
1 ½ cups heavy whipping cream
2-3 tablespoons powdered sugar, optional
Vanilla ice cream
Fresh nutmeg

Shortcake
2 cups all-purpose flour
1 tablespoon baking powder
½ teaspoon salt
3 tablespoons sugar
1 stick cold butter, cut into small cubes, plus
3 tablespoons butter, melted
⅔ cup whole milk, plus extra if needed

1. Slice strawberries and toss in a bowl with sugar, if needed. Keep covered in refrigerator until needed.
2. In a large bowl, beat whipping cream until soft peaks form, add powdered sugar to desired sweetness, then continue beating until stiff peaks form. Keep covered in refrigerator until needed.
3. Preheat oven to 425° F.
4. To make shortcakes, combine flour, baking powder, salt, and sugar. Add butter, and then, using a pastry cutter or forks, mix with flour until mixture resembles small peas.
5. Make a well in center of mixture and add milk. Stir together just until combined. Do not overwork dough. Dough will be sticky.
6. Line a baking sheet with parchment paper and using an ice cream scoop, drop dough onto sheet, about 3 tablespoons in each scoop. Brush tops with melted butter and bake for 10-12 minutes, until tops are golden brown.
7. Let shortcakes cool before assembling with ice cream and strawberries.
8. Shave fresh nutmeg over the tops and serve.

Peach Crisp
Serves 10-12

10 peaches, sliced
½ cup brown sugar
¼ cup cornstarch
1 teaspoon SplenDishes Pumpkin Pie Blend

Topping
1 cup all-purpose flour
1 cup brown sugar
½ cup quick cooking oats
1 teaspoon baking powder
½ teaspoon SplenDishes Pumpkin Pie Blend
Pinch of salt
½ cup cold butter

1. Preheat oven to 375° F.
2. Place peaches in greased baking dish. Sprinkle with brown sugar, cornstarch, and Pumpkin Pie Blend and gently toss.
3. In a bowl, combine flour, brown sugar, oats, baking powder, salt, and Pumpkin Pie Blend. Cut in cold butter until mixture resembles coarse crumbles. Sprinkle over peaches and bake for 45 minutes until golden and bubbling.

Want Wine?

Wine pairing suggestion:
Rosé

Wine notes for similiar choice:
Fruit forward with dryness helps cut the sweetness.

Blackberry Cobbler
Makes 4 ramekins

3 cups blackberries, plus extra few for garnish
2 tablespoons cornstarch
2 tablespoons coconut sugar,
  plus extra for sprinkling
Pinch salt
2 tablespoons butter, diced
2 puff pastry sheets
½ cup butter, softened (not melted)
½ cup brown sugar
¼ cup almonds, sliced and toasted
Pinch salt
1 egg, beaten
Vanilla ice cream

1. Preheat oven to 400° F.
2. Mix together berries, cornstarch, coconut
   sugar, salt, and butter in a bowl. Spoon into
   lightly greased 3 inch ramekins.
3. Place ramekins on lined baking sheet.
4. In another bowl, combine softened butter, brown
   sugar, almonds, and salt. Mixture should be the
   consistency to spread (not melted). Sprinkle
   evenly on the tops of berries in each ramekin.
5. On a lightly floured surface, take each puff
   pastry sheet and lightly roll out pastry to
   approximately ¼ inch thickness. Cut into
   rounds that are same size as the ramekins.
6. Place pastry circles on top of berries and sugar
   mixture in ramekin, and brush with egg mixture.
   Sprinkle tops of pastry with coconut sugar.
7. Bake at 400° F for approximately 20-25 minutes,
   or until pastry is puffed and golden brown.
8. Serve with vanilla ice cream and extra berries.

Want Wine?

Wine pairing suggestion:
Zinfandel

Wine notes for similiar choice:
*Dark fruits like blackberry
with a hint of spice contrasts
the sweetness.*

CHEF-INSPIRED
STAGIONI

Executive Chef Andrew Dodd
Stagioni

After working just a few months in the kitchen at Stagioni: Four Seasons of Food, Bruce Moffett promoted Andrew Dodd to Executive Chef in Summer 2015.

A native of Nashville, Tennessee, Dodd's first job in a kitchen was dishwasher at 15 years old. He worked his way up to cooking, and fell in love with the "controlled chaos" that he calls a restaurant kitchen. He worked in kitchens in Seattle, Spokane, and Boston before moving to Charlotte in 2007 to begin school at Johnson & Wales University. Shortly thereafter, he began working at one of Charlotte's most exclusive and upscale restaurants of that time, Ratcliffe on the Green. He became sous chef there, then spent four years as Executive Chef of George's Brasserie.

Dodd planned on taking a break from the kitchen in late 2014, then came along the chance to work for award-winning chef Bruce Moffett at his third Charlotte restaurant, Stagioni. "Working for Bruce is kind of like a wish list item," he said of his new opportunity. Six months later, Bruce promoted Dodd to Executive Chef. Dodd describes Italian cooking as "a respect for ingredients." That respect he shares for fresh, locally-sourced ingredients, coupled with his Southern-influenced cooking style, prove to be the perfect match for Stagioni and Moffett Restaurant Group.

Stagioni is the third restaurant for Bruce Moffett of the Moffett Restaurant Group in Charlotte, North Carolina. The restaurant lies in a historic landmark known as "The Villa"; it is actually the Reynolds-Gourmajenko house that has a long and interesting history. Mrs. Blanche Reynolds Gourmanjenko, a world traveler, who married a Russian émigré during a tour in Europe, built the city's only Tuscan villa. She spared no expense on the interior design. The furniture and materials used in the build out stay true to the history of the The Villa. There is even a picture of Blanche's son's wedding from 1954.

Stuffed Squash Blossoms
Serves approximately 10-15 for appetizers

2-3 dozen Squash Blossoms (depending on size,
  pistil removed)
1 cup cream cheese (softened)
½ cup mascarpone cheese (softened)
½ cup grated parmesan cheese
½ cup jumbo lump crab meat
½ cup fine diced bell peppers and onions (lightly
  sautéed and cooled)
½ cup fine diced zucchini and yellow squash
  (seeded, lightly sautéed, and cooled)
1 tablespoon fine-diced chives
1 tablespoon fine-diced parsley
1 tablespoon salt (may take more to taste)
1 teaspoon black pepper

1. Mix all ingredients except for crab very
   thoroughly. Once all incorporated, add crab
   and fold in gently as too not break up crab
   chunks. Store refrigerated in pastry/piping
   bag. Once chilled, slightly cut ¾ inch opening
   in bag. Using tip of the bag, insert filling into
   blossoms and refrigerate.

Prosecco Batter

¾ cup of all-purpose flour
¾ cup tapioca flour
1 tablespoon salt
1 ½ teaspoon baking powder
1 cup prosecco wine
1 cup seltzer water

1. Preheat fryer to 350° F.
2. Mix dry ingredients first, then add wet
   ingredients. Batter should be the consistency
   of loose pancake batter. Grab each blossom
   by the stem and dip into batter, then slowly
   drop into fryer, gently shaking back and
   forth. Cook on one side, about 3 minutes,
   using tongs to flip and cook on other side for
   2 minutes. Remove from oil and drain on
   paper towels.
3. Serve with chive aioli and red pepper jelly.

Want Wine?

Wine pairing suggestion:
Chardonnay

Wine notes for similiar choice:
*The oak and dryness compliments
the earthiness of the dish.*

There's no doubt I have good taste in bartenders! On any given day, you can walk into Stagioni and find Russ behind the bar. He's hard to miss, tall and handsome with this amazing head of hair and well-groomed beard. He'll mix you up one of his mouth watering libations or simply pour you a lovely glass of Italian wine. His signature cocktail, the Fresco 1926, is right up my alley. It has vodka, lemon lime shrub, Cointreau®, fresh lemon and lime juice, and a red wine float. It is so delicious, so watch out because they go down fast!

Bartender Brian "Russ" Johnson
Stagioni

Brian "Russ" Johnson is a North Carolina native, and has traveled extensively around the world, expounding upon and perfecting his craft. His favorite drink to make is the one you want. His motto is "... give me a fruit, a flavor, or a destination, and I can make you a drink!"

INDEX

ACKNOWLEDGEMENTS

Thank you to my family. To my husband, Eric who always has my back and supports everything I put my mind to, and always kills it on the grill, and my daughter, Shaiyla who inspires me every day.

To my dad, Gary Pugh, or OD as I call him, my biggest fan and supporter, and my favorite uncle, Dr. Indrojit Singh. Without you both, this book would have never happened.

To my amazing business partner and friend Su Kelley, you make working fun and have put the cooking sparkle back in my eye.

To my second right hand, Tamara Ashlock, thank you for always knowing which direction to put me in.

To Jennifer Moore, you're the best rock a girl can have, thank you for always being there and having my back.

You girls may shadow me on this cover, but you certainly shine light on my life, otherwise.

To Jenifer Sutherland, who is like a second mother to my daughter, I couldn't do my job without you. We are blessed to have you in our family.

To Lisa Reyes Nalbach and Aaron Matthew Melton of The Color Bar Hair Salon, for always getting my hair and makeup TV Star ready.

CPSIA information can be obtained at www.ICGtesting.com
Printed in the USA
BVIW12n1000021217
501501BV00027B/151